God's Kind of Love
A Journey of the Heart

Dr. Bob Abramson

God's Kind of Love - A Journey of the Heart
Author: Dr. Bob Abramson
Published by Alphabet Resources, Inc.
365 Stonehenge Drive
Phillipsburg, NJ 08865
1-561-963-0778

Dr.Bob@mentoringministry.com

Cover design by Ryan Stacey - Visual Lion

13 digit ISBN 978-0-9846580-2-2

Contact Dr. Abramson by visiting
www.mentoringministry.com.

Table of Contents

◌ֆ৪৩ Preface ◌ֆ৪৩

I have spent quite a number of years thinking about God's kind of love, reflecting on what it is. It has led me to ask myself if I have it; and, whether it reflects in how I live and how I love. I am not sure that I can yet answer these questions to my satisfaction. The book you are about to read is my attempt at this.

When I began this book, I thought it would be relatively simple to write. Was I surprised! It has taken me over three and a half years to write it. This is not because the book is lengthy. It is not because the subject seemed to be particularly difficult. After all this time, I have discovered that I probably could keep writing and editing it for the rest of my life. The subject is far too big for me to encapsulate in the pages that follow. I am convinced that God's kind of love is the essence of His nature. Therefore, it is so vast and multifaceted that it is beyond any earthly attempt to record it fully in a book. Nevertheless, I believe that what follows can be your open door to the same kind of life's journey I am taking. With all its unexpected turns, my life is a walk on a path of discovery about who God is and what His love means to me. As you begin, join me and let your life's journey center on discovering the same.

☙ Introduction ❧

This book is about love as God practices it, and His Word defines it. In 1 John 4:11, the Apostle John tells us, *"...if God so loved us, we also ought to love one another."* In the original Greek language of this text, John's word for *"love"* is *"agape."* He writes that God is *"agape"* and that we are to *"agape"* one another. *"Agape"* is God's kind of love. It is both a reflection of the person of God and the actions of the Godhead. *"Agape"* is used at least three hundred and twenty times in the New Testament. God considers His kind of love of the utmost importance. Indeed, it is one of His divine attributes. He does not view His command to *"agape"* or *"love"* one another as a suggestion. It is one of His most clearly communicated commands in the New Testament. It comes directly from Jesus. He meant it to be a reflection of His heart at work in ours.

Matthew 22:36-40 (NKJV)

""Teacher, which is the great commandment in the law?" {37} Jesus said to him, "'You shall love the LORD your God with all your heart, with all your soul, and with all your mind.' {38} This is the first and great commandment. {39} And the second is like it: 'You shall love your neighbor as yourself.' {40} On these two commandments hang all the Law and the Prophets."

3

The scriptural intent of *"agape,"* points us to action. We are to love according to God's perspective. This demands that our actions fit His definition and expectations. He built us to thrive on His kind of love. It is part of our original design. It is His workmanship in us. At times, however, we fail to understand its intent and value. There are those of us who simply do not know how to love or be loved. Some of us are just not equipped for it. We use the word, "love" in many ways, with many implied meanings. We say, *"I love you,"* or *"I love pizza,"* or *"I love to swim,"* or *"I love my mother."*

For some, love is elusive. They search for it and never find it. Others think they have found it, only to see it disappoint them and slip from their grasp. Their lives are incomplete and lacking in that one thing needed by everyone - God's kind of love. Here are three examples of love we commonly find in our societies. These inevitably fail to satisfy, because they are not God's kind of love (*"agape"*).

Love as Intense Uncontrollable Feelings

For some people, love can be a series of intense, uncontrollable feelings (emphasis on "uncontrollable"). What they commonly think of as love is actually an emotional search for something that never satisfies. It always seems to be out of reach. Their search for love becomes an abuse of the genuine meaning of *"agape."* It is a counterfeit of the real thing. It leads to disappointment and emotional damage. Thinking they have found love, because it delivers this series of feelings and experiences, can be misleading and confusing. For these people, life is out of control. They watch themselves being moved in and out of love, without an expectation that there is anything they can do about it. The consequences are inevitably negative, whatever they may be. The feelings are genuine, but fail to meet the requirements of God's kind of love. These feelings deliver nothing but negatives. The once hoped for positives that could have been mutually shared, expressed and maintained are missing. Ultimately, love as intense, uncontrollable feelings is far from being beneficial to those who are parties to it. They come to know it as a trap or a curse.

Love as Intense Controlling Feelings

There are those who experience what they believe to be love as a series of intense, controlling feelings (emphasis on the word "controlling"). They find they have lost personal control over the direction of their lives. They have become slaves to their feelings. When it comes to extracting themselves from the damage of these controlling emotions, they cannot see how to do it. They feel forced into the journey without any relief. Life for them is like being in a boat in a fast moving river without oars, motor or anchor. Someone or something else has the rudder. It seemed right to begin with, but now its direction and speed is wrong. It is impossible to stop, and the damage is in the process of being done. This too, is not God's kind of love. Notice how both uncontrollable and controlling feelings have nothing to do with what their victims know. They are captured by what they feel.

Love as Both Uncontrollable and Controlling Feelings at the Same Time

In this category, we find people entangled in what they first thought was love. However, they have found themselves in the unfortunate position of being manipulated by feelings that are both uncontrollable and controlling. They are trapped in the misfortune of simultaneously experiencing the worst of our two previous examples, combined. They are captive to their feelings, and unable to find a way out. They experience a sense of helplessness and have become targets for emotional damage. They become like puppets on a string. Something is pulling at them and they feel as if they are without control. Everything about their "love" relationship is determined by the way, and with whom their circumstances have evolved. Obviously, this is not God's kind of love either. Notice that all three of these counterfeit "love" types operate within a person's feelings.

The Remedy

The remedy for all three experiences with what the world calls "love" lies within what I will share with you in the pages that follow. We will enter into what the Scriptures present us as guidance into God's kind of love or *"agape."* This inevitably can lead to God's will for your life, which is the peace, joy and strength found in *"agape."* As we begin the chapters of this book, I will share with you some of my experiences in ministry and life. In these, I found the meaning, and embraced the expression, of God's kind of love (His *"agape"*). You will read how it changed my life. I will do my best to give you biblical principles of God's kind of love, with which you can guide your personal path through life. Proceed through the pages of the book with an open heart and mind. The Holy Spirit will bring you all you need to become all God has designed you to be - a successful and significant dispenser of God's kind of love.

1 Corinthians 13:8a (NKJV)

"Love never fails..."

Redemptive Love

The verses of Scripture with which we began in Matthew Chapter 22, record what ought to be understood as the most significant desire of the Lord Jesus Christ for anyone who follows Him. Again, He said this:

> *"'You shall love the LORD your God with all your heart, with all your soul, and with all your mind.' {38} This is the first and great commandment. {39} And the second is like it: 'You shall love your neighbor as yourself.' {40} On these two commandments hang all the Law and the Prophets.'"*[1]

Jesus' preeminent command is that we are to love the Lord with everything in us. Nothing is to be held back. Nothing is more important. Nothing that comes from within us is to be more full of impact than our love for God. Jesus' second commandment, which is like the first, is that we are to love others as we love ourselves. I have found this a bit puzzling, as not all of us have love for ourselves. The weight of sin or

---

[1] Also recorded in Mark 12:28-33 and Luke 10:25-27.

the sorrows of failure, and even the words of others have molded our views and self-perceptions falsely. In order to love others, we may need change the way we look at ourselves.

As followers of Christ, we are redeemed from the damage this world has done to our self-images. Redemption released us to be people whose lights shine with the image of Christ. Redemption allowed us to embrace, for ourselves, God's view of us as born-again, God fearing, God serving people.

When you gave your heart to Jesus, the debt against you was not simply canceled, but was forever paid in full. Christ's blood was the essence of His earthly life. He surrendered it at the cross. It became the "ransom" He paid that completely delivered you and me from slavery to sin, with all its eternal consequences.

Hebrews 9:12 (NKJV)

"Not with the blood of goats and calves, but with His own blood He entered the Most Holy Place once for all, having obtained eternal redemption."

The Lord Jesus Christ had the singular goal of our redemption in His heart from the moment the three members of the Godhead agreed upon the divine plan they established in eternity past. It was plan of love - God's kind of love. It required the ultimate act of love, the separation of one of the three divine Persons from the others. It had to be done in the darkest way, and it was. On a hill named Golgotha, the Lord Jesus Christ was forsaken and left to die the most horrible of deaths. Jesus knew how costly the love-driven gift of our redemption would be to Him. He was the One to pay the price. One of my Bible school students, Tara McConnell, put it this way, as she reflected on her own salvation with this colorful description.

> *"My life wasn't my own, I was enslaved by my sin. I was like an animal chained and caged with no freedom anywhere in sight. Sitting on a hill, my rusty, locked cage sat, sealed shut by my evil master. I had earned my imprisonment from the start, my release was nowhere in sight. I had no ability to obtain liberation from that cage. As I stood longing for deliverance, a Man ascended the hill. He told me He bought my freedom. He paid my ransom and my chains were broken. My cage door was opened. He was my new Master."*

Loving the Lord with all we are and loving our neighbors through our redeemed self-images are not divine suggestions. They are commands from heaven. Christians are to judge and validate every other commandment by these two. Jesus demonstrated this in His conversation with the rich young ruler.

Matthew 19:16-19 (NKJV)

> *"Now, behold, one came and said to Him, "Good" Teacher, what good thing shall I do that I may have eternal life" {17} So He said to him, "Why do you call Me good? No one is good but One, that is, God. But if you want to enter into life, keep the commandments." He said to Him,*

"Which ones?" Jesus said, "'You shall not murder,' 'You shall not commit adultery,' 'You shall not steal,' 'You shall not bear false witness,' {19} 'Honor your father and your mother,' and, 'You shall love your neighbor as yourself.'"

In John's Gospel, Jesus made a significant statement that reinforced his answer to the rich young ruler.

John 14:15 (NKJV)

"If you love Me, keep My commandments."

Our redemption has opened the door to freedom. We have the opportunity to display this freedom in our obedience to God's commandment to love. I have found from experience that when God commands us to do (or not to do) something, He does so out of love for us. Our freedom, along with its ability to provide us with success and significance, depends upon our obedience to His commands.

John 8:36 (NKJV)

"Therefore if the Son makes you free, you shall be free indeed."

ᘓᔥ 1 ᘓᔥ

God's Kind of Love: Abiding Love

1 John 4:16 (NKJV)

"And we have known and believed the love that God has for us. God is love, and he who abides in love abides in God, and God in him."

One of the clearest descriptions of how God views love comes from one of our church fathers, St. Augustine. When describing the love relationship within the divine Trinity, he wrote this.

"Love involves a lover, a beloved, and a spirit of love between the lover and the loved. The Father might be likened to the lover; the Son to the loved one, and the Holy Spirit is the Spirit of love."[2]

St. Augustine's description of love, using the example of the three Persons of the Trinity, illustrates love's primary characteristic. It is completely relational in its quality and function. In its simplest form, love (*"agape"* or God's kind of love) is a connection that is mutually shared, expressed

---

[2] "The Relational Disciple," © 2010 Joel Comiskey. Published by CCS Publishing, Moreno Valley, CA, P. 38.

11

and maintained, while being beneficial to all involved. The motivation for this connection is found throughout John's writings. In His Epistle of 1 John, he tells us why we should love one another. It is clearly stated.

1 John 4:7-11 (ICB)

"Dear friends, we should love each other, because love comes from God. The person who loves has become God's child and knows God. {8} Whoever does not love does not know God, because God is love. {9} This is how God showed his love to us: He sent his only Son into the world to give us life through him. {10} True love is God's love for us, not our love for God. God sent his Son to be the way to take away our sins. {11} That is how much God loved us, dear friends! So we also must love each other."

The "punch line" or teaching point of this passage is found in Verses 10 and 11. It presents us with a cause and effect lesson. The cause is God sending Jesus to *"take away our sins."* The effect this demands of us is that *"we must also love each other."* It is the classic example of Scripture confirming Scripture. John confirms the Lord's command to love our neighbors as ourselves. He equates God's kind of love to God's kind of sacrifice.

There is a Scottish legend about two unmarried sisters who had such a bitter argument that they stopped speaking to each other. Though they were unwilling to reconcile, they continued to live together in their small home. As you read this story, reflect on the necessity and the value of God's kind of abiding love.

There were two unmarried sisters, who had lived together all their lives. They had a bitter argument. Because of the argument, they stopped speaking to each other. One of the sisters drew a chalk line to divide their one-room home into two halves. The line went from the doorway all the way to the fireplace at the other end of the room. This allowed each of them to come and go without any interaction with the other. Each could get her own meals without trespassing on her sister's domain. In the black of the night, each could hear the breathing of the other. For all the years of their lives, they coexisted in grinding silence. Neither was willing to take the first step to reconciliation. They died alone and lonely. Even though they lived close enough to hear each other breathing in the night, they never had the comfort of each other's presence.[3]

Again: *1 John 4:8 (ICB)*

"Whoever does not love does not know God, because God is love"

In September of 2008, my wife Nancy and I found ourselves returning to the city of Malacca, in the nation of Malaysia. We were there once again to teach at the Chinese-language Bible School, which is part of Agape Renewal Center. What followed was a busy and tiring three weeks. Now, it was the

---

[3] Stevenson, Robert Louis, Edinburgh, Picturesque Notes by Robert Louis Stevenson, People's Edition, London Seeley & Co, London, 1903, Chapter 4.

final evening before we would leave for our next assignment in Taiwan. On this final night, I was preaching at a local Chinese church. Our students from the Bible school were present in the congregation. It was normal and expected in that part of the world that a visiting speaker would spend considerable time praying for people at the conclusion of the service. However, I was wiped out, as I was incredibly spent from the effort of the last three weeks. I did not think I had much left in me to do anything more than pray a short closing prayer. I should have known better. As usual, God was full of surprises.

As I began my closing prayer, I felt the presence of God so strongly that I could have melted right where I stood. I looked at the congregation, and my heart filled with love for them. It was not simply an emotion I was feeling, but something more. The presence of God was tangible. His love permeated the church. I experienced a sense of understanding that God loved them so much more than I possibly could. My heart broke wide open. God would not leave them in the condition they were in, and neither could I. I stepped down from the pulpit and began inviting people to come to the altar to receive prayer. We formed them into two lines. I prayed on one side of the church and my wife, Nancy prayed on the other. It was apparent that nobody was leaving the church until we had prayed for everyone there.

As I prayed, I became aware of the special quality of the moment. I knew the congregation was receiving something far more than I had to give them. God was touching them with His kind of love. In many ways, it was as if I were merely a spectator. I watched as the people were being enveloped by the fullness of God's grace and love. Many were overwhelmed by it. I certainly was. It energized me, and I waded in, praying with increasingly great fervor. Any consciousness of my fatigue had disappeared. It was a moment when all of us experienced something special - the special kind of love that God can deliver so completely. It was God's abiding love. It was God.

Again: *1 John 4:16 (NKJV)*

"And we have known and believed the love that God has for us. God is love, and he who abides in love abides in God, and God in him."

Since that time in Malacca, and especially because of the experience of that final evening service, I have not been able to escape the demanding reality of God's kind of abiding love in my life. Though I went to Malaysia with an academic agenda, I found that God had a more important reason for Nancy and me to be there. He brought me to Malacca to discover the depths and limitless impact of His loving care and concern for people. From that moment, the way I view God's call on my life has plumbed new depths in my heart. I am forever changed. Let me tell you what happened at the altars in that Malaysian church during that final service. It begins with a Malaysian Chinese young man, who was a student in the Bible school in Malacca. His English name is Johnny.

Johnny was unmarried and in his late twenties. He had given himself over to the call to ministry. It required sacrifice and a not-so-easy walk of faith. When Nancy and I had first arrived in Malacca, I noticed Johnny almost immediately. Though he was not assigned to do so, he would accompany the student who came to pick us up each morning from where we were staying, and they would drive us to the school. Johnny came along, just to ask questions and be around us as much as he could. He also came to our hotel one afternoon with other students. I sat in the lobby with them, talking about many things pertaining to ministry. When it comes to seeing the call from God to become a pastor, I have a good sense of recognition. I saw that it was all over Johnny. He wore it like a glove.

Now, let me take you back to our final evening service in Malaysia. Nancy and I continued to pray for our two lines of people. It was very late. I had been praying for quite some time. Once again, I felt close to being overwhelmed by the fatigue that was creeping in. Finally, Johnny approached me, as he was next in line. This was to be the final time I would interact with him during my trip there. As he came forward, I asked him what I could pray about for him. He said something I could never forget.

> *"Would you pray that I could receive the same love for people in my heart that you have shown us."*

It was one of those moments when I was driven to the depths of humility. I was undone. I was taken completely back by what Johnny said. I looked at him in silence for a few moments. Then I embraced him and gave him a big hug while I prayed something like this.

> *"Father, give Johnny the gift of seeing people through eyes of your kind of love. Let it so permeate*

him that it defines his life and ministry. Let Johnny have a double portion of whatever he sees that you placed in me. Thank you Lord for using him to shine his light with your love, in Jesus name. Amen."

As I prayed for him, Johnny began to weep. He could not stop. He just clung to me as the tears flowed. Then, he slipped to the floor and lay there crying. His were tears of joy. I realized that something was being released from heaven. It was received into his heart. I am sure that in that moment Johnny got one of the greatest gifts any of us could receive from God. He was infused with the reality of God's kind of love. Amazingly, so was I. God had sovereignly forged the moment into something special neither of us would forget. That night, we both went away from the meeting changed forever. Let me share with you a principle that my experience in Malacca taught me.

Define Yourself with God's Abiding Love.

So much of the world tries to invade our lives and persuade (and even control) our choices. I encourage you to allow yourself to seek, and then be guided by God's abiding love at every turn of your life. In 1 Corinthians 13:8, Paul wrote, *"love never fails."* God, who is love, never fails. His guidance is always correct and fully accurate. It is synchronized with His abiding love.

I have learned that if you look first to His kind of love, you can walk in step with it, in full confidence that He is your ever-present, unfailing Guide. I strive to make doing so a habit, a ready response to the things I face from day to day. I am doing my best to walk with Him in this special kind of abiding, loving guidance that only His presence can provide. I wish I could always be successful in doing so, but it is a deliberate choice that must be made repeatedly. The guidance God's kind of love brings will do what nothing else can. It will shape and guide your character. It will determine your path in life. It will influence and change those you touch as only love can do. Embrace it. Let it fill your path with good success and true eternal significance. Let God's abiding kind of love shine from you.

In the Most Unlikely Places

Christ's ways are never hit and miss. It is supposed to be the same with each of us. He has not called us to stagger randomly through life. Your path is entwined purposefully with the paths of others. The Lord has deliberately designed you to be part of a living, interactive community - His church. When you seek the Lord, you will find Him in your relationships with others of like faith. When you seek His purpose for your life, you will find much of it in your interactions with others. Often, it will be with believers, but He will also ask you to go beyond your church community to those who have no community. He will provide you with the opportunity to invite them into the family of God.

Christ is out there waiting for you in the most unlikely places, among the most unlovely people. In Matthew 25:40, Jesus calls them *"the least of these my brethren."* Be prepared to look into the faces of these people. He has given them to you. See them through the eyes of compassion. See them through eyes filled with God's kind of love. Welcome them and offer them your hand of fellowship. You will go to places in God you otherwise never could. You will find Jesus in these people. They are the least of His brethren, but great in His heart. Do this and you will find Him profoundly up close to, and personal with you.

Matthew 25:37b-40 (NKJV)

"'...Lord, when did we see You hungry and feed You, or thirsty and give You drink? {38} When did we see You a stranger and take You in, or naked and clothe You? {39} Or when did we see You sick, or in prison, and come to You?' {40} And the King will answer and say to them, 'Assuredly, I say to you, inasmuch as you did it to one of the least of these My brethren, you did it to Me.'"

It was the year 2000. We had established a church on Roosevelt Island, in the East River, between Manhattan and Queens in New York City. It was during this time I was offered the opportunity to also pastor a small Baptist church in Queens. I explained I was not a Baptist and there could be some doctrinal issues, but they looked past that and seemed determined that I was the one for the job. After some prayer and considerable discussion, Nancy and I added this little church to our already busy schedule. I felt I did the right thing by accepting the call to this church, but had no idea why I should do so. It only took a few weeks to understand why this happened.

There was a lovely lady in the church. She had welcomed us as pastors with a warm heart and open arms. She was grateful for us and we were equally grateful for her. Shortly after we settled into the task of pastoring this second church, we learned that this precious lady was diagnosed with an advanced case of inoperable cancer. There were three things my wife, Nancy and I knew we could do. First, we could pray for and with her. Second, we could believe God for her healing. Third, we could show her God's abiding love. We would do whatever our part was to make His love a powerful force in her life. She eventually succumbed to the disease and it was my great privilege to preach her funeral. It was not long afterward that we were able to transition the ministry in the church to a Baptist pastor. To this day, I am certain that she was the reason God placed us there.

The experience showed me how our willingness to embrace God's people and pour out His abiding love invades even the most dreadful of times. I came to the realization that we were sent there for that short time, so we could walk with that lovely, gracious, faith-filled lady through her final days on earth, until she went straight into the arms of Her Savior. I know how tenderly and significantly we touched her heart. I believe she surely touched ours a thousand times more. God provided that season of sorrow and turned it into memories of sad, yet joyful understanding. Indeed, God's kind of love never fails. It always accomplishes something within those who embrace it. It always brings a display of His glory.

Matthew 5:14-16 (NKJV)

"You are the light of the world. A city that is set on a hill cannot be hidden. {15} Nor do they

light a lamp and put it under a basket, but on a lampstand, and it gives light to all who are in the house. {16} Let your light so shine before men, that they may see your good works and glorify your Father in heaven."

Ephesians 5:2 (NKJV)

"And walk in love, as Christ also has loved us and given Himself for us, an offering and a sacrifice to God for a sweet-smelling aroma."

The Least of These My Brethren

John 5:5-8 (NKJV)

"Now a certain man was there who had an infirmity thirty-eight years. {6} When Jesus saw him lying there, and knew that he already had been in that condition a long time, He said to him, "Do you want to be made well?" {7} The sick man answered Him, "Sir, I have no man to put me into the pool when the water is stirred up; but while I am coming, another steps down before me." {8} Jesus said to him, "Rise, take up your bed and walk.""

I can remember when I began to pastor the Christian Mission Fellowship International Church in Fiji. God provided us with a great meeting room for our church. It was on the upper floor of a two story commercial building in the heart of Suva (Fiji's capitol city). The roof leaked buckets of water every time it rained and there was no air conditioning to relieve the heat. However, we all loved the place. We not only had beautiful times of worship there, but we established the denomination's School of Urban Missions. Here we trained so many incredible men and women, who were subsequently sent across the world with the Gospel message.

It happened that, because our building was located in the heart of downtown Suva, we were directly in the place where streetwalkers, thieves, beggars and homeless people hung out. Every morning at ten o'clock, we took a break from teaching in our ministry training school. We all had tea and whatever snacks we could manage. Money was scarce, but there was always something good to share. I watched my students grow and become more like Jesus every day. They soon could not avoid thinking of these beautiful, down and out people who could be found on the sidewalks all around our building. They began to invite them up to join us for tea. They put no pressure on them. They were just welcomed with God's kind of love. I do not really know if this changed any of them. I pray that it did. I know that it changed my students, and we all became just a little bit more like Jesus, every day in some little way.

Again: *John 5:7b (NKJV)*

"Sir, I have no man to put me into the pool..."

Matthew 25:37-40 (NKJV)

"Then the righteous will answer Him, saying, 'Lord, when did we see You hungry and feed You, or thirsty and give You drink? {38} When did we see You a stranger and take You in, or naked and clothe You? {39} Or when did we see You sick, or in prison, and come to You?' {40} And the King will answer and say to them, 'Assuredly, I say to you, inasmuch as you did it to one of the least of these My brethren, you did it to Me.'"

Jesus habitually modeled a heart for the downtrodden, the sick and the helpless. They are precious to Him. Yet, how often are we reluctant to take the risk, suffer some inconvenience or even unpleasantness to answer the call to see Jesus in them? Fulfill your responsibility. You may be perhaps the only measure of Christ they will encounter. Give what you have of yourself to someone who is waiting for a stirring of the waters, but waits without hope. As you do, you just might find you ministered to the Lord.

Who is Your Neighbor?

Luke 10:29b-37(NKJV)

"And who is my neighbor?" {30} Then Jesus answered and said: "A certain man went down from Jerusalem to Jericho, and fell among thieves, who stripped him of his clothing, wounded him, and departed, leaving him half dead. {31} Now by chance a certain priest came down that road. And when he saw him, he passed by on the other side. {32} Likewise a Levite, when he arrived at the place, came and looked, and passed by on the other side. {33} But a certain Samaritan, as he journeyed, came where he was. And when he saw him, he had compassion. {34} So he went to him and bandaged his wounds, pouring on oil and wine; and he set him on his own animal, brought him to an inn, and took care of him. {35} On the next day, when he departed, he took out two denarii, gave them to the innkeeper, and said to

him, 'Take care of him; and whatever more you spend, when I come again, I will repay you.' {36} So which of these three do you think was neighbor to him who fell among the thieves?" {37} And he said, "He who showed mercy on him." Then Jesus said to him, "Go and do likewise.""

In addition to being the capitol of Fiji, Suva is also the home of the University of the South Pacific. Our church attracted many students from the many cultures represented at the university. It was a joy to look out from my pulpit and see such a variety of faces in our young people. The multicultural nature of our church attracted others who lived and worked in the city and wanted to be part of this diverse fellowship. For the better part of the first year, there were no American faces in our church. My wife Nancy and I loved the multiculturalism, and were perfectly comfortable and pleased with the variety of people in attendance. However, we missed the fellowship of other Americans. We just kept praying for some American friends with whom we could share familiar experiences. One day, I looked up from my pulpit and saw a couple with their five children walk in the door. They were apparently Americans. As the service ended, we confirmed this in a conversation with them. They were Mark and Lynn Roche and their children. What a joy! God had answered our prayers with this wonderful family.

Mark, Lynn, and their children, had come to Fiji to develop a safe place for young, single mothers and their children, who had been abandoned or abused. Some had been threatened, thrown out into the streets and had no alternatives except begging or prostitution. It took very little time for me to see that God's kind of love was just dripping from Mark and Lynn's lives. Their ministry began with what seemed insignificant. They took one young woman and her small child off the streets and into their home. They lived primarily by faith and had little in the way of personal comforts. Their story is amazing. In time, they helped this one young woman become educated, go to the university and find a good future for herself and her young son. She was simply the beginning.

At this writing, it has been about sixteen years since the Roche family first walked into our church. Their ministry, "Homes of Hope, Fiji," now has a beautiful campus in the hills outside of Suva. It has become a home, a sanctuary and a training ground. It is a place where many, like that first young lady and her son from the streets, are rescued, housed, trained and given a future. The campus is a testimony to the Lord's heart for the downtrodden. It is a place where Jesus reigns. It is a safe, loving place. Now the Roche family is working toward branching out to the other countries of the South Pacific and Africa. In these other places, they and others who have come along side them, will surely find Jesus in the faces of *"the least of these My brethren."* I know they have made a great difference in so many people. I also know that they have experienced Christ as few of us can. God's kind of love pours out of their lives and ministry. It is an inspiration and a beautiful thing to behold.

Most of us are not called to a lifetime of commitment and sacrifice at such a high level as the Roches. However, we all can search our hearts and ask ourselves if we desire to experience the same kind of Christ-like love that first penetrated and then moved the Roches. For the majority of God's people, it is not going to require a move of thousands of miles. However, it can become our opportunity to move immeasurably closer to God. We can become a little bit more like Jesus every day.

Principles for Loving as God Loves

1. People who love as God loves attract others who also learn to love as God loves.

   Demonstrate Christ. Let your light shine. You will not be alone for long in your walk with God. He will provide others to walk with you. It may take a while for them to come, but trust God that His timing is never off. Somebody is waiting on the other side of your obedience. Just keep obeying His commandment to love with His kind of love.

2. People who love like God loves attract people who do not know love, have not been loved and cannot yet love.

   God's kind of love becomes a magnet to those who have not experienced it, have lost it, or have rejected it. God's kind of love is stronger than any emotion because it is not an emotion. It is a decision, packed with power from on high.

Matthew 11:28-30 (NKJV)

"Come to Me, all you who labor and are heavy laden, and I will give you rest. {29} Take My yoke upon you and learn from Me, for I am

gentle and lowly in heart, and you will find rest for your souls. {30} For My yoke is easy and My burden is light."

3. People who love like God loves are change agents.

They attract those whose lives can be transformed from hopelessness and helplessness into something radically different. The hopeless and the helpless can become vessels, lovingly fit for the Master's use. The Apostle Paul understood this truth. He wrote this in 1 Corinthians 11:1 (NKJV). *"Imitate me, just as I also imitate Christ."*

4. People who love like God loves attract great resistance to their love. It comes from the evil one.

Resistance comes from the dark powers at work trying to prevent God's love from its appointed purpose. This purpose is to be your appointed (and anointed) purpose. Go ahead and let your light shine. Let it release those who are downtrodden and sorrowing, through a demonstration of God's kind of love. Doing so will define your life and become your great opportunity. You are a difference maker, waiting to make a difference.

1 John 4:4 (NKJV)

"You are of God, little children, and have overcome them, because He who is in you is greater than he who is in the world."

Within you is the ability to demonstrate God's kind of love. To do so is to demonstrate God's kind of power. Neither of these can be defeated. You are dangerous to the devil and all his schemes, plans and efforts. Walk in love and you will put him under your feet.

Ephesians 5:2 (NKJV)

"And walk in love, as Christ also has loved us and given Himself for us, an offering and a sacrifice to God for a sweet-smelling aroma."

5. People who love like God loves cannot out-give God.

God will faithfully multiply the love you give away to others. It will happen, not only in, through, and to them, but you will come to know His love in ways that are indescribable and ever-increasing. Seek His face in the needy faces of those you will touch. God is waiting for you in them. Again, they are *"the least of these My brethren."* Love them and you will be loving Him. He will respond with an infusion of particularly powerful love, straight from His heart to yours.

6. People who love like God loves have eternal significance.

In my years of being a Christian, I have observed that the only lasting satisfaction we get is when our lives demonstrate something eternally significant that finds its way into others' lives. Only a demonstration of God's kind of love can bring this about.

- Take your love beyond its emotional boundaries.
- Look for eternity in your choices to be like Jesus to others.
- Carry an awareness of the impact and effect your words, actions, attitudes and deeds will have. Ask yourself whether they will have eternity in them? Ask

yourself whether they will allow eternity with Christ to flow out of them into others? The answers to these two questions are the stuff from which an eternity of blessings is made.

∞ 3 ∞

We are Nothing without Love.

It is widely accepted that the Apostle Paul established the Corinthian church on his second missionary journey (about 51 A.D.). A few years later, on his third missionary journey, while in Ephesus, Paul received a report that greatly disturbed him. It compelled him to write his First Epistle to the Corinthians. He wrote this letter to address the problems and pressures of his Corinthian brothers and sisters' life-styles. Corinth was notoriously immoral. The people of the church had taken on much of the city's cultural negatives. Some had brought these ungodly ways into the church body, as new believers. Others had returned to many of the sinful cultural norms of the city they had forsaken when they were saved. Paul first addressed the Corinthians' sinful ways. Then, in Chapter 13, he turned to providing them with an understanding of God's sinless, holy kind of love.

1 Corinthians 13:1-3 (NKJV)

"Though I speak with the tongues of men and of angels, but have not love, I have become sounding brass or a clanging cymbal. {2} And though I have the gift of prophecy, and understand all mysteries and all knowledge, and though I have all faith, so that I could remove

*mountains, but have not love, I am nothing. {3}
And though I bestow all my goods to feed the
poor, and though I give my body to be burned,
but have not love, it profits me nothing."*

As we proceed through this chapter, we will unpack these
first three verses of 1 Corinthians 13. Together, they speak
of the futility of attempting to do the works of Christianity,
without loving as God loves. Paul writes about the
meaninglessness of Christian life when it is void of love. Let
us look at these three verses.

1 Corinthians 13:1 (NKJV)

*"Though I speak with the tongues of men and of
angels, but have not love, I have become
sounding brass or a clanging cymbal."*

Be sure to notice that Paul used himself as the example
(*"Though I speak..."*). He often used this technique to
deflect any emotional rejection of what he had to say. He
wrote to the Corinthians as their brother in Christ, with
equally human weaknesses and faults. Paul's message is
clear from the beginning of the chapter. Regardless of whom
the speaker is, even if an angel, his or her words are empty
sounds unless they are empowered by and filled with God's
kind of love.

Paul employed the sound of percussion instruments for his
contrasting imagery. These instruments make harsh, loud
sounds. They are incapable of playing the kinds of beautiful
melodies that bless a person's soul. They have no ability to
soothe or put people at ease. Like these percussion

instruments, our words can become brash and harsh without love. When empty and loveless, our words define our identities. They illuminate our souls. They give evidence that we are brash, harsh, unloving people.

Now, let us go on to the second verse in Paul's "love chapter." It is the companion to the first, but takes the imagery further and makes a profound statement to us.

1 Corinthians 13:2 (NKJV)

"And though I have the gift of prophecy, and understand all mysteries and all knowledge, and though I have all faith, so that I could remove mountains, but have not love, I am nothing."

In this second verse, Paul, again used himself as the example. He went beyond describing himself without love as a cold, hard percussion instrument. Now his example of himself without love is something of infinitely less substance. He writes, *"...but have not love, I am nothing."* What could be less than *"nothing"*? Obviously, nothing is the ultimate absence of anything. It can be likened to the same formlessness and void that God spoke to when He created the universe (Genesis 1:2). Paul brings to mind this emptiness, with words that describe the condition of a person living without God's kind of love.

In Verse 2, Paul provided us with a list of incredibly valuable gifts (prophecy, wisdom and even mountain-moving faith). He used them to show that life does not find its meaning in what we are capable of doing. Only when we are defined by what we are capable of being, which embodies and displays the personal attribute of God's kind of love, do we have eternal value to those around us. Paul knew that his fruitfulness and value was never really about what he did. It was always about who he was. I have said many times that if we become who we are capable of being, we will do what we are called to do. In the first book I published, "Just a Little Bit More - the Heart of a Mentor," I repeatedly encouraged the reader to become *Just a little bit more like Jesus.* I would encourage you to strive to become the same, with every opportunity, and in every way you can. You will become a living epistle, and people will read the life-changing story of God's kind of love in your story.

Paul's examples of prophecy, wisdom and faith in Verse 2 cover a wide spectrum of a Christian's life. However, without God's kind of love infused in us, our gifts are not worth as much as *a sounding brass or clanging cymbal.* They are nothing. Reflect on this and then, take a studied look into the mirror. Whom do you see? What do you hear? See and hear yourself as God does. He sees your potential. You have the God-given potential to be a great influence and blessing for Jesus - just a little bit more each day and in every way.

Let us move on to 1 Corinthians 13:3. I have provided two translations below; the New King James Version and the International Children's Bible.

1 Corinthians 13:3 (NKJV)

"And though I bestow all my goods to feed the poor, and though I give my body to be burned, but have not love, it profits me nothing."

"I may give everything I have to feed the poor. And I may even give my body as an offering to be burned. But I gain nothing by doing these things if I do not have love."

In Verse 3, Paul showed himself again to be sensitive to the emotions of the Corinthian brothers and sisters. He tempered his rebuke for a third time by using himself as the example. He wrote of sacrifices that range from his giving up personal possessions to feed the poor, to the most difficult and personal of sacrifices, which is to be burned to death. The punch line or unexpected turn in this verse is powerful - *"But I gain nothing by doing these things if I do not have love."* This was meant to have an immediate effect on his readers. Let me paraphrase Paul's words for you.

My Paraphrase of 1 Corinthians 13:3

I want you to know that whatever I (Paul) may sacrifice, from something as minor as giving up what I have to feed the poor, to something much more profound and costly, I am talking about giving everything and enduring anything, including an excruciating death for the sake of the Gospel. It will all be less than nothing, unless it is filled with, and empowered by God's kind of love.

Paul was consumed with the love God had given him. He desperately wanted the Corinthian church to grasp the fullness of the same love that God showed them. He has stated his case three ways. First, without God's kind of love, whatever Paul does makes him no better than an empty noise. Second, regardless of what he does, knows or believes, without God's kind of love, he is nothing - a complete dark void. Finally, whatever happens because of him or to him is meaningless without God's kind of love within him. This is because he gains nothing that would contribute to his purpose or fruitfulness. Together, these three pictures converge in the minds of his readers to deliver the message. Without God's kind of love, we are empty, absent and unfulfilled during our brief times on earth. With it we can be all God designed us to be and can do all that is in His heart to make a difference among those He gives us, whom we are to love and care for.

Paul has now prepared his readers for what he has to say about *"agape,"* or God's kind of love, in the remainder of Chapter 13. He will write of how love operates in the life of the believer. He will offer the reader nine things that love does, mixed with eight that it does not do. As you continue to read, you will see that I have chosen to major on the nine positives, while not dwelling on the negatives. These positives become guidelines to our Christian walk. They are keys to a successful and eternally significant journey through life. They are as follows.

Love...
    Verse 4: *"suffers long"*
              "is kind"
    Verse 5: *"thinks no evil"*
    Verse 6: *"rejoices in the truth"*
    Verse 7: *"bears all things"*
              "believes all things"

> *"hopes all things"*
> *"endures all things*
Verse 8: *"never fails."*

It is fitting that Paul finished his list with this assurance that *"Love never fails."*

C380 4 C380

Love with Patience.

1 Corinthians 13:4a (NKJV)

"Love suffers long..."

1 Corinthians 13:4a (NIV)

"Love is patient,"

If you were to examine the original Greek text of the first characteristic of love (1 Corinthians 13:4), you would find it translates into English as, *"Love suffers, suffers."* There is a word picture painted here of repeated acts of patience, even though they may be painful to endure. The words of the Greek text describe a longsuffering love that is given patiently, habitually and sacrificially. This is God's kind of love. It is characterized by a passionate and determined concern for the person being loved.

The practice of patient love is a profoundly positive exercise and experience. It speaks of a God-given capacity for self-control, despite the circumstances, trials or tests. The degree of patience you show will be determined by the degree of Christ in the attitudes of your heart. It will be reflected in the relationships in your life.

Colossians 1:10-11 (NKJV)

"that you may walk worthy of the Lord, fully pleasing Him, being fruitful in every good work and increasing in the knowledge of God; {11} strengthened with all might, according to His glorious power, for all patience and longsuffering with joy;"

Colossians 1:11b (NIV)

"...so that you may have great endurance and patience..."

In the years I pastored in Fiji, it was my habit to spend a lot of time in my study at my home. It afforded me a measure of privacy and quiet that allowed me to engage myself with uninterrupted time in God's Word. It was a great environment to prepare lessons for our School of Urban Missions or training sessions for the church leadership. It was especially important for me to have undisturbed time to study for my Sunday sermons at the church. One afternoon, I was hard at work in my study preparing a sermon for Sunday's service. Interestingly enough, it was on the subject of love. I have since reflected on the goodness of God to put what seem to be random acts or events together for His divine purposes. Let me illustrate this observation for you.

As I was deeply engrossed in preparing my Sunday sermon, I heard a knock at our front door. My wife, Nancy, answered it. She found a group of our students standing there with containers full of food. As was the habit of Fijians, they came unannounced to bless us with their fellowship and spend the afternoon in our company. Nancy, of course, was immediately delighted and invited them in.

I heard all of this as I sat in my study. It distracted me from what I was working on. I was immediately irritated at the interruption and disappointed that I could probably not continue with my work. It was at this moment that I learned two things. First, disappointment is always an opportunity for another appointment, an appointment with God. Second, when we have appointments with God, they are teachable moments that usually include the presence of others. I was about to have my appointment!

Nancy came into my study and announced the inevitable. *"Your students are here and they have brought us food. They are waiting for you in the living room."* Well, this was not news to me. I had expected her words. I grudgingly closed my Bible and the incomplete computer file on my "love" sermon that I had been writing. This moment was the beginning of an appointment that would be profoundly and personally teachable - for me. It would surprise me and radically change my life. Never forget that there are no surprises in heaven, but always plenty of surprises from heaven. Every one of them is good.

It happened in a flash. As I walked out of my study into the living room, I was preparing to put on an artificially happy face to greet my students. From my first glance at them, my whole world turned upside down. I was apprehended and struck with regret, conviction and compassion as if it were a lightning bolt. God spoke to my spirit and said something like this.

43

These students are My gift to you. They are full of My love for you. Now is the time for you to go beyond what you can do and learn about what you can become.

My life changed forever. I went out into the midst of all this love and spent the afternoon with my wonderful students. It was a time filled with God's kind of love. It was the beginning of a journey that has continued to this day. By the way, my sermon that Sunday was glorious. Now, that is not the end of the story. Here is the next part.

As I am writing this, some fifteen years later, I am sitting at my computer alone in our home in Florida. My wife is visiting with my mother-in-law, who is at this moment in a rehab center, recovering from a fall. (She will be fine and I am grateful to God.) Just before I typed this paragraph that you now read, the phone rang in the kitchen. I was irritated at the interruption. I grudgingly left the computer and answered it. (Does this sound familiar?) It was my wife. She was calling to report on the good progress my mother-in-law was making.

Wow! Here I was, sanctimoniously writing about the power that God's kind of love touched me with so many years ago. God interrupted me to reinforce, in another powerfully teachable moment, that the people I loved and cared for, who had the same feelings for me, were still so much more important than a book, or a sermon or a lesson. Ouch! I was struck with the same kind of lightning that hit me that first time back in my home in Fiji. I must wrap it up with this paragraph, as, at the time of this writing, I am on my way to visit my lovely and most wonderful gift from God, my mother-in-law, Ruth.

At times, it is easy to fall back into the same habits we try so hard to change. I could not leave writing of the previous two instances about which you just read, without reporting a third. It happened as I was engaged in editing a book I have written called, "Focused on the Father - The Lord's Prayers." As I was working on my computer, doing the editing, the phone rang. It was one of my young pastors in training who needed advice. I listened with some irritation; quickly gave the advice and told him I was busy with my editing. I asked him to call me later. The moment I ended the call, I knew I had repeated that old pattern of sinful disregard for someone who was infinitely more important than a few words in a computer file. I immediately called the young man and apologized. He had not taken offense. Nevertheless, I knew I had done the wrong thing. God's kind of love is too precious to put at a lower priority. I should have yielded to the needs of the young man.

Principles for Loving Patiently

1. People who love patiently are a demonstration of Christ.

   Christ waits patiently for us to come to Him in our sins and sorrows. He does not get impatient or mean-spirited. He just loves us, always at the ready to move into our situations without condemning us. His only motivation is that His kind of love would free us from what has us bound.

2. People who love patiently find their patience protects them from impulsive mistakes.

Part of our human nature is that we are impulsive. We respond quickly to the dictates of our emotions and natural thinking. Patience is a virtue that yields great rewards.

James 1:2-4 (NKJV)

"My brethren, count it all joy when you fall into various trials, {3} knowing that the testing of your faith produces patience. {4} But let patience have its perfect work, that you may be perfect and complete, lacking nothing."

The Scriptures are true. They translate into every day life as encouraging messages filled with God's kind of love. My paraphrase of James 1:2-4 reads like this. Let these words sink deeply into your heart.

In every trial and test, be joyful. You can do this because you understand that the things you go through test your faith, which produces the patience that will keep you from making mistakes. Just let your experiences help you to grow. When the test or trial is finished, you will be equipped for what God has next for you.

3. People who love patiently are rewarded by God for their willingness to wait.

Include God in your waiting process. He will act on your behalf and change the situation. In the process, He will strengthen your resolve and enhance your ability to do things His way. He is waiting for the opportunity to display the power of His faithfulness through your life.

Take a moment and reflect on the words of Isaiah, below. He asks an interesting question.

Isaiah 40:28-31 (NKJV)

"Have you not known? Have you not heard? The everlasting God, the LORD, The Creator of the ends of the earth, Neither faints nor is weary. His understanding is unsearchable. {29} He gives power to the weak, And to those who have no might He increases strength. {30} Even the youths shall faint and be weary, And the young men shall utterly fall, {31} But those who wait on the LORD Shall renew their strength; They shall mount up with wings like eagles, They shall run and not be weary, They shall walk and not faint."

4. People who love patiently find they will have more patience with their own imperfections and weaknesses.

   I can testify that this is true for me. I had long been impatient with others who did not measure up to my expectations. As I allowed God's kind of love to soften my attitudes, I found that not only did my patience toward others increase, but I no longer was so hard on myself. I have learned to live more peacefully with my own shortcomings and imperfections. You might find this helpful to break through the limitations imposed by your own feelings. You cannot patiently love others without it causing you to be more lovingly patient with yourself. (The reverse is true too.)

5. People who love patiently give themselves time to see the true character and intentions of those around them.

There will be occasions when our first impressions are not correct. Time has a way of revealing truths that are initially hidden. It also has a way of revealing lies that have been hidden. The application of loving patiently will provide you with the wisdom to make correct judgments about the character and intentions of others. This is especially true for those with whom you share the intimate experiences of your life.

6. People who love patiently provide others with a sense of safety and security.

God will use your loving patience to give people a sense of well-being. You become the facilitator of His peace through your words and actions (and often, your inactions or ability to wait). They will sense the Lord at work in you and be calmed and assured by your demeanor. Your calmness can become theirs. They can catch the attitudes found in your loving patience and be sustained through troubling times.

God's kind of love, patiently working in you, will build your strength, your character, and give you wisdom. It will provide you with a platform for peaceful living. Then, you will become someone God will use to make a difference in the world around you. As you have seen, *"Love never fails."*

Love with Kindness.

1 Corinthians 13:4a (NKJV)

"Love suffers long and is kind,"

To be kind is to be considerate, compassionate, good-hearted, giving, supportive, empathetic, warm and tender. When you love with kindness, you are giving unselfishly to bless others. You become an imitator of Christ, who gave unselfishly of Himself. Your presence becomes the place where His grace will flow. Richly warming experiences will come to those to whom you show kindness, because you have allowed the flow of heavenly grace to be unhindered, as it comes through you. That is God's kind of love.

Ephesians 4:32 (NKJV)

"And be kind to one another, tenderhearted, forgiving one another, just as God in Christ forgave you."

My paraphrase of Ephesians 4:32

And be sure to love each other with benevolent consideration and tenderness. Be sure that you are ready to forgive, and take deliberate action to do so. Always keep in mind that God in

Christ was ready to forgive you. Forgiveness of others is the least you can do.

It is amazing how one person's decision to show loving kindness can change the world around him or her. Consider this story as a gift from my heart to yours. When I first read of it, I was so touched I have never forgotten it. I have since told it to many people in various places around the world. I read about it in Dr. Joseph Stowell's terrific book, "Shepherding the Church."[4] In it, he writes of an encounter he had on an elevator in the Administration Building of Moody Bible Institute, during the time he was its president. Here is a recap of what he wrote.

> Dr. Stowell was getting in an elevator one day on the way to his office on the ninth floor. The elevator doors were made of stainless steel and easily showed fingerprints. A woman from the housekeeping staff regularly rode the elevators to keep the doors clean. This woman got on the elevator as the doors were closing and began to clean them. She was struggling because she could not reach the top of the doors. As Dr. Stowell watched her, he was struck with the reality that Christ had come to serve. He asked the lady if he could take the rag and spray bottle to get the part she could not reach. With a startled look, she handed them to him. As Dr. Stowall began to clean the doors, the elevator stopped and some students got on. He kept cleaning the doors and

[4] Stowell, Joseph M., Shepherding the Church, © 1994, Victor Books/SP Publications; © 1997, Joseph M. Stowell, Moody Press, Chicago, P. 135.

finished before he got off. A few weeks later, he asked the housekeeper how cleaning the elevator doors was coming along. She said, *"Just fine; in fact, lots of people are helping me now."*

Loving with kindness becomes a magnet that draws others to do the same. They catch the love that comes out of your heart and it begins to flow out of theirs.

The love that Dr. Stowell demonstrated may be translated into a kindness that goes beyond our natural instincts or thinking. It becomes a spiritually led, life-changing action. His elevator cleaning proved two things. First, the principles of Romans 12:2 are still valid. We can all change our thinking to reflect the goodness and perfect will of the Lord.

Romans 12:2 (NLT)

"Don't copy the behavior and customs of this world, but let God transform you into a new person by changing the way you think. Then you will know what God wants you to do, and you will know how good and pleasing and perfect his will really is."

Second, Dr. Stowell's demonstration proved that loving kindness in action will communicate a convicting, liberating effect to those who are watching. Dr. Stowell's consideration for the housekeeper was a perfect picture of the heart of Christ, who came to serve, rather than being served. As the students watched Dr. Stowell clean those doors, they heard the Holy Spirit speaking within their hearts. They listened and learned. Then, they engaged themselves in a transformation that brought a demonstration. It was a demonstration of loving kindness. Thank God for the opportunities to clean elevator doors, or whatever else God puts in our hearts.

One of the things that I try to bring forward in my thinking is to look compassionately at those I encounter. Compassion brings the joy of knowing that, just at the right moment, you can reach someone's heart with actions that secure, comfort and encourage them. Compassion works to attract people to the Christ in you. As it does, your world can open up far beyond any natural or earthly expectation. Dr. Stowell's elevator cleaning example went much higher than the ninth floor of Moody Bible Institute. It climbed the clouds and touched heaven. Your example can do the same.

Loving "without" Kindness

The commandment is to love with kindness. This suggests that what people mistake for love can be an act done "without" kindness. All too often, what people call love is an act of gross misunderstanding. Let me explain in the following ways.

1. What might be thought of as an act of love can be merely something done out of a sense of obligation. For example, a person may not have real concern for the well-being of someone with whom they are interacting. Theirs may be a false portrayal of love, because people are expecting it to be given. They may feel that if they do not provide what appears to be love, their reputation or standing among others will be minimized. When this

occurs, it is not an act of kindness. It is loving "without" kindness.

2. What might be thought of as an act of love can be a selfish attempt to gain something. This is deliberate manipulation, hidden behind a lack of transparency. In these instances, the display of love is a counterfeit. It may be done with great skill, but it is a lie. It uses someone's pain, misfortune or need to further the counterfeiter's own desires. This application of what people commonly mistake for love is often seen in those who try to excuse their sins of abuse, neglect or infidelity.

3. What might be thought of as love can be a display of tolerance for someone's sinful position or actions. The person who assumes a tolerant posture, in the name of "love," becomes an enabler of the other person's sinful behavior. This can happen because of a lack of biblical knowledge or lack of understanding of the truth. The result will not please God. It will neither justify nor make a way of escape for the one caught in the sin. Instead, it merely strengthens their bondage to the sin. Nowhere in God's word is tolerance for any kind of sin justified or encouraged. Tolerance is not kindness. It is another counterfeit of love. It is a sin. If you feel tolerant, measure your feelings against God's plumb line of righteousness.

As you can see from the examples above, what commonly and mistakenly is identified as love can be given "without" kindness. In every case, the outcome fails to edify or lift the person into a better place. To love with kindness requires a clear understanding of God's kind of love. Consider these three characteristics of God's kind of love.

- It is unselfish, sacrificial and giving.
- It has no motive for personal gain.
- It is determined to bring about a twofold outcome. (1) It will lift a person to a better place. (2) It will bring to them a demonstration of the goodness of God. Hopefully, (and this is between them and God) it will draw them closer to God.

Random Acts of Kindness

There will be times when the kindness and character of Christ will show itself in you, without an intentional effort on your part to display it. This happens when you see others with a softened, compassionate heart. In these times, it is the little things, that seem almost instinctive, that will make the difference. To you, they may seem to be nothing special, but you never know what they mean to someone who receives God's kind of love from your actions. Let me give you an example that seemed to be nothing special to me, but then spoke so loudly to my heart that I have never forgotten it.

Some years ago, I was standing in the checkout line at a big electronics retailer. In front of me were two people. One was a little boy, who stood all by himself in the line. The other was a young man about twenty years of age. I cannot remember what the little boy was buying, but, as the clerk rang up the sale, I noticed that it cost about ten dollars. The boy reached in his pocket and started counting his money. After a bit, it was obvious that he was a few dollars short of the price he needed to pay.

There was a prolonged pause, as the little boy displayed a disappointed and hurtful expression on his face. In this awkward moment, I decided to provide the money he needed. However, before I could, the young man in front of me took his own money and paid the balance needed. The little boy beamed with joy and away he went with his prize.

That moment in the checkout line was one of those in which God provided me the opportunity to observe His loving kindness in action. It was a teachable moment. I often think that God prevented me from providing the little boy the money he needed. I believe He did so to teach me a vital lesson about discernment. Here is what I learned. There will be times when your compassion moves you to take action without fully discerning the situation. In the case of the checkout line, God must have wanted the young man standing in front of me to provide the money. Had I impulsively stepped in, trying to be the benefactor, I would have robbed him of his opportunity to be a blessing. I might have robbed this young man of much more.

I can only speculate how that young man in line ahead of me felt; and how providing the necessary money might have spoken to his heart. This I do know. God always knows who is appointed for the task at hand. As I wrote earlier, there are no surprises in heaven, but I learned that there will be great surprises from heaven. I took a great piece of revelation away from that checkout line.

Before you act, give God time to speak to your heart. Let Him show you the broader picture and direct your steps one way or the other. You just might be surprised. You can be sure that whatever He surprises you with will be good. Oh, there is one more thing. In God's kingdom, random acts of kindness that demonstrate His kind of love are never actually random. They always have within them, a divinely designed purpose and a divinely designated person. Even so, God depends on our discernment to keep the way clear for these acts to happen.

Deliberate Acts of Kindness

A deliberate act of kindness is one that is carefully considered. It weighs the implications and outcomes it will generate. It is a purposeful decision. For someone who tries to walk in the will of God, its purpose should be first, that it pleases God. Then, that it gives a positive, edifying and fruitful result for those it affects. It should always be governed by a heart of compassion, filled with God's kind of love. Personal cost may be an issue, but if the cause is just, cost ought not to be a barrier or excuse. Kindness in loving action is a sure sign of someone who desires to honor God with his or her life.

Deliberate acts of kindness should be done with compassion. Do so with God's kind of love. Fill your heart with forgiveness and wrap it in tenderness. You never know how the outcomes of your actions might change others' attitudes, and perhaps even their lives.

Principles for Loving with Kindness

1. Consider loving with kindness to be a divine door opener to the intimate presence of God.

Regardless of whether it is planned or seems randomly to be given, loving with kindness is always an opportunity for someone to experience the presence of God. Earlier, I wrote, "You will find Jesus in these, the least of His brethren. You will find Him profoundly up close and personal." Let these words touch your heart once more.

Jesus was consistently clear on this subject. If you want to receive an invitation to experience Him at the deepest level, look for Him in your acts of loving kindness toward those who others would ignore or neglect. This principle is equally true for those close to you.

2. Consider loving with kindness to be more than simply an opportunity. Consider it an obligation.

Every one of us, who has experienced the undeserved and unmerited gift of salvation, ought to take ownership of the obligations that come with it. We should often remind ourselves of the Lord's words to Peter, recorded in Luke, Chapter 12. What Jesus said remains a universal truth, regardless of time or place.

Luke 12:48b (NKJV)

"... For everyone to whom much is given, from him much will be required."

3. Consider loving with kindness to be more than an opportunity or obligation. Consider it to be your strong tower.

You may not experience immediate relief from a particular discomforting circumstance. However, you may be certain that if you have walked in God's kind of love, you will experience an eternally dependable release from the grip of unpleasant circumstances that may temporarily take hold of you. God will not forsake you. He will see you through and join with you in the experience. You will find that, in your willing display of His kind of love, He is truly your strong tower.

Years ago, I was fighting a battle with life-threatening cancer. I was under a probable death sentence spoken by the doctor. I had nowhere to turn but to lean on Jesus. In those moments, I chose to draw closer to Him. I determined to love Him more, in the midst of my pain. I made the determination that I would also show God's kind of love to the medical professionals who cared for me. I would not, and did not ever complain. I simply witnessed to the goodness and dependability to God. I never gave the devil and inch! I gave everything to Jesus.

I can testify that the Lord created a divine bubble for me within which I could abide. The singular characteristic of this bubble was Christ's assurance of His presence and His response to my need. Though the journey was filled with uncertainty and pain, it was also filled with the certainty of my salvation and the joy of the Lord. I knew I was in a strong tower. There, I found perfect peace. I knew I was in the light. It was not just at the end of my tunnel, but continually in the tunnel with me. I made it through because of the loving, powerful presence of God. In the end, I received my release from the death sentence and a shower of God's refreshing touch.

Proverbs 18:10 (NKJV)

"The name of the LORD is a strong tower;
The righteous run to it and are safe."

I have committed Psalm 46 to memory. It is a great reservoir of comfort, always available to me. Here are a few verses.

Psalms 46:1-2, 7 (NKJV)

"God is our refuge and strength, A very present help in trouble. {2} Therefore we will not fear, Even though the earth be removed, And though the mountains be carried into the midst of the sea... {7} The LORD of hosts is with us; The God of Jacob is our refuge. Selah"

4. You can make loving with kindness someone else's strong tower. This happens when you are a reflection of the Christ in you. They may not understand, but God will delegate you to point the way for them to find Him as their strong tower. Loving with kindness has the potential to become far more than an act of compassion in action. It has the potential to become the most power-packed evangelism tool there is. When others see you in action, their eyes could be opened and they might just be seeing Jesus in action. Their salvation may be your reward.

How can you incorporate loving with kindness into your daily life so it makes a difference to those around you? This is a question worth the attention of every one of us.

೧೮ 6 ೧೮

Love while Rejoicing in the Truth.

1 Corinthians 13:6b (NKJV)

(Love) "...rejoices in the truth,"

This is my paraphrase of this part of Verse 6.

> *God's kind of love celebrates the truth that His Word and divine presence have revealed.*

To rejoice means to immerse your heart in a celebration of what is taking place. It is to make merry and take the celebration to its extreme, because of the magnitude of what has happened. The Apostle Paul wrote the following, as he connected rejoicing, prayer and thanksgiving.

1 Thessalonians 5:16-18 (NKJV)

> *"Rejoice always, {17} pray without ceasing, {18} in everything give thanks; for this is the will of God in Christ Jesus for you."*

Notice the short, concise emphasis in these three verses. Paul described these as the will of God for us. Let us look at each of the three in the light of 1 Corinthians 13:6. What connections might we find to God's kind of love?

1. *"Rejoice always."* (Verse 16)

What is it that makes it possible to *"rejoice always,"* regardless of what the moment brings? The answer is in the ever-present truth we have from 1 Corinthians 13:6b, with which we began this chapter. It says that love *"rejoices in the truth."* In the midst of the worst imaginable trials and troubles, this connection remains rock-steady and unmovable. Under the heaviest of burdens, it enables us to be free to keep our eyes and hearts on Jesus. He is the truth. In John 8:32, the Lord said that we would *"know the truth"* (both our knowledge of Him and our intimate, personal relationship with Him) and it would set us free. This gives us the freedom to rise above whatever we face, while rejoicing in the God of our salvation.

Acts 16:22-26 records that while in Philippi with Silas, the Apostle Paul cast a demon out of a slave girl who was possessed by a spirit of divination. She told fortunes to make money for her masters. Once freed from the evil spirit, she could no longer do this. Therefore, her masters seized Paul and Silas, dragged them into the marketplace and had them beaten and thrown into jail. As you read through these Scriptures, you will find Paul and Silas praying and singing hymns to God. In the midst of their miserable situation, they were rejoicing in the Lord and having sweet fellowship with Him. Their situation did not stop them from celebrating the joy of their love for God. As they sang, a powerful response came from heaven. Their chains were broken and the prison doors were flung open by an earthquake. Then, they walked out. Here is the scriptural account of this event.

Acts 16:22-26 (NKJV)

"Then the multitude rose up together against them; and the magistrates tore off their clothes and commanded them to be beaten with rods. {23} And when they had laid many stripes on them, they threw them into prison, commanding the jailer to keep them securely. {24} Having received such a charge, he put them into the inner prison and fastened their feet in the stocks. {25} But at midnight Paul and Silas were praying and singing hymns to God, and the prisoners were listening to them. {26} Suddenly there was a great earthquake, so that the foundations of the prison were shaken; and immediately all the doors were opened and everyone's chains were loosed."

God honored Paul and Silas' demonstration of love toward Him with His faithful, liberating response. Then He used this display of the power of His love to touch the hearts of the jailer and his family with salvation. Now they too, could rejoice in the truth of God's kind of love. This leads me to relate to you a testimony of my own rejoicing and liberation from a different kind of prison.

In the previous chapter, I told you about my battle with life-threatening cancer, and how the Lord was my strong tower. Let me share a little more from that experience. It might help illuminate further how Paul and Silas could rejoice, while still in their painful imprisonment in the Philippian jail.

There were times during my fight with cancer that I was captive to continuous, intense pain. I will not go into details about why this was happening, except to tell you it was directly related to complications from treating the cancer I was fighting. I frequently found myself in the emergency room of New York Hospital, Queens.

On one particular occasion in the emergency room, the pain was so intense that I could not bear it. The doctor treating me did not seem concerned with my pain. In fact, I felt like he was the devil himself in a hospital coat. (Of course, that was not the case.) As I lay there, I suddenly felt the comfort of the Holy Spirit envelop me. I cannot explain this, except that it was God's kind of love straight from heaven, invading my suffering. The excruciating pain was still there, yet, I knew I could rejoice... and I did. I experienced the privilege of suffering in the company of the Lord! The Apostle Paul called this the *"fellowship of His sufferings."*

Philippians 3:8, 10-11 (NKJV)

"Yet indeed I also count all things loss for the excellence of the knowledge of Christ Jesus my Lord, for whom I have suffered the loss of all things, and count them as rubbish, that I may gain Christ... {10} that I may know Him and the power of His resurrection, and the fellowship of His sufferings, being conformed to

*His death, {11} if, by any means, I may attain to
the resurrection from the dead."*

In other times that followed, until Christ healed me, I
experienced more of the same fellowship. It gave me an
understanding of how someone can be falling under the
weight of persecution, pain or suffering, and yet, rejoice.

Philippians 4:4-5 (NKJV)

*"Rejoice in the Lord always. Again I will say,
rejoice! {5} Let your gentleness be known to all
men. The Lord is at hand."*

Yes, I have learned, in all things, to *"Rejoice always."* I
can do this because *"(Love)* *"rejoices in the truth.""* It
has set me free. I have often said, you can argue with
many things, but you will never successfully argue with
a person's experience. What you just read was one of my
most awesome experiences with rejoicing in the truth of
God's kind of love. Never doubt that regardless of what
you may face, *"the Lord is at hand."*

2. *"...pray without ceasing."* (1 Thessalonians 5:17)

Paul wrote this verse to encourage his Thessalonian
brothers and sisters to continue in a lifestyle of
communion and communication with God. It is not
complicated or filled with hidden meaning. The
Amplified Bible Paraphrase of this verse says, *"Be
unceasing in prayer [praying perseveringly]."* Paul,
because of his own experiences serving Jesus, knew the
value and necessity of determined, persevering prayer. It
has to be a way of life, in which we always give

preeminence to God. Paul reminded the Thessalonian church that persevering and unceasing in prayer would draw them nearer to God. James, in his epistle, tells us that God faithfully responds to this, by drawing closer to His children (James 4:8). As the Thessalonians continued to pray, God would be with them in all of their circumstances.

Praying *"without ceasing"* is a sure prescription for God's redemptive presence. It is a great tool we have been given to shape a future of good success, in the presence of the only One who can guarantee it for us.

3. *"...in everything give thanks."* (1 Thessalonians 5:18)

It was shortly after my wife, Nancy and I had moved to New York City to establish a new church. Little did we know how difficult it could be living in this vast, unfamiliar city. Living there was costly and the culture of the city was as foreign to us as any we encountered on the mission field overseas. This made for a steep learning curve. It required determination and effort, as we began our church planting activities.

We could not afford expensive living quarters, but God provided us with a small apartment in Queens, just two blocks from a Long Island Railroad station. We soon became very thankful for this apartment. It was a place of peace and provided us with security and comfort. The location also provided us with easy access to Manhattan, where we were working to plant our church. It was a great neighborhood with shops and beautiful, tree-lined streets. The apartment was owned by two lovely elderly

Jamaican ladies, who lived on the floor above us. Most Saturdays, they would go to a store in Jamaica, Queens, and bring us tasty Jamaican patties and loaves of delicious Jamaican bread. They would even invite us to dinner on occasion. We soon looked upon them as family. These two precious ladies were God's gift to us.

One thing I will never forget is that they provided us with a parking place. (Unless you have lived in New York City and have had to search for a place to park your car for the night, you may not appreciate what a blessing this was.) They did this at the expense of having to park their own car on the street. At first, I do not think I understood what a sacrificial blessing this was. It was their pure expression of God's kind of love, given unselfishly and without expectation of any return or advantage to them. I will always be thankful, especially when I recall so many cold winter nights when we returned home late and did not have to search for a parking place on the street, because the driveway was always awaiting our return.

It was my habit to take my morning prayer-walks around the neighborhood. I did this in the sunshine, the rain or snow. These were times when God would really speak to me. (He has a way of doing this with perfect timing.) One morning, I was out walking and praying. It was a beautiful, clear day. It had been a difficult week, as is frequently the case for church planters. As I walked, I was engaged in a personal pity party. I was thinking about the conditions in which we lived. I was comparing them to how many of my friends and family lived, who were not called to missions as we were. My thoughts were stuck on how nice it would be if only we had a real house of our own. Poor Bob. What a pity!

Suddenly, it happened. As I walked down a particularly beautiful street, the Holy Spirit spoke to my heart. Though it was spoken in silence, its message was loud and clear. It shattered my pity into pieces. He said, *"Look around. See all the beautiful houses I have given you to enjoy as you walk with Me."* I knew He meant that all these great houses I walked by were positioned as part of His plan for my prayer path. What a gift! From that moment on, each day as I walked, I enjoyed looking at my great New York houses and thanked God for my beautiful prayer path. I rejoiced in the truth that He had prepared it because of His love for me. Yes, it was God's kind of love, and He personally demonstrated it to me, just when I needed a wakeup call.

At times, we all lose our joy. When this happens, we easily lose sight of our connection to God's kind of love, for which we ought to be thankful. Perhaps you need a wakeup call as I did. Below is a truth in which you can rejoice. It will make a way for your joy to return, along with a renewed sense of gratefulness to God.

> *Thankfulness to God is the lens through which we discover the blessings we otherwise would not see. God provides us more than enough reasons to be thankful in everything.*

ᘓᔐ 7 ᘓᔐ

Love with a Protective Heart.

1 Corinthians 13:7a (NKJV)

(Love) "...bears all things."

1 Corinthians 13:7a (NIV)

"It always protects."

The original Hebrew word for *"bears" or "protects"* means *"to cover with silence"* and *"endure patiently"*[5] while doing so. To protect or cover means to guard, care for, shelter, watch over and keep others safe. Therefore, we could paraphrase *(Love) "always protects""* in this way.

> *God's kind of love (agape) in action is fully dependable. It will patiently guard and shelter God's people from whatever would harm them.*

Loving others in a way that *"always protects"* is a costly effort. It usually requires a shift in priorities from what pleases "me" to what is best for "them." As with the other aspects of God's kind of love I have shared with you, this one is a decision to forego personal comfort, advantage or desires, in favor of doing what is necessary for the well-

---

[5] Strong's Concordance, through Parson's Technology - QuickVerse, Number G4722.

being of others. When we love others, we are actually loving Christ. Knowing this should not be our motivation, but it does place profound meaning on the act of demonstrating God's kind of love, regardless of how inconvenient it is to do so, or to whom it is done.

One of the finest examples of choosing God's kind of love over any personal advantage or agenda is found in the Book of Ruth. Ruth and her mother-in-law Naomi had experienced tragedy. Following the deaths of their husbands, they journeyed together back to Naomi's home in Bethlehem. They had no means of support, and no way of caring for themselves.

Ruth found herself gleaning in the fields of a relative of Naomi, whose name was Boaz. He showed her kindness by allowing her to glean in his fields, and instructing his workers to leave extra grain for her. He also ordered them to watch over her and keep her safe while she was in the fields. This led to an encounter between Ruth and Boaz during harvest time. It was a pure illustration of love operating with a protective heart. Here is what happened.

Ruth 3:7-11 (NKJV)

"And after Boaz had eaten and drunk, and his heart was cheerful, he went to lie down at the end of the heap of grain; and she came softly, uncovered his feet, and lay down. {8} Now it happened at midnight that the man was startled, and turned himself; and there, a woman was lying at his feet. {9} And he said,

"Who are you?" So she answered, "I am Ruth, your maidservant. Take your maidservant under your wing, for you are a close relative." {10} Then he said, "Blessed are you of the LORD, my daughter! For you have shown more kindness at the end than at the beginning, in that you did not go after young men, whether poor or rich. {11} And now, my daughter, do not fear. I will do for you all that you request, for all the people of my town know that you are a virtuous woman.""

From this biblical illustration, we can glean the following principles about how *"God's kind of love (agape) in action is fully dependable..."* to *"patiently guard, and shelter God's people from whatever would harm them."*[6]

1. God's kind of love seeks no advantage over others. It flows out of a tender heart. It acts to give the person who is at a disadvantage an advantage. It protects regardless of what might be gained from doing otherwise.

   Boaz enjoyed a position in which he easily could have abused his power over Ruth, both earlier in his fields and then in the night she came to him at the threshing floor (Ruth 2:8-12 and 3:7-11). He chose to look upon her with tender mercies in his heart. His motives were pure before God. He was a man whose character reflected God's kind of love.

---

[6] Taken from Page 69.

2. God's kind of love can reveal itself in our refusal to submit to our natural human temptations. Instead, we allow our choices to be filled with righteous protection.

Love allows us to submit our carnal reactions to the spiritual leadership of the Holy Spirit. Boaz did this on that night in the threshing floor. Ruth was completely vulnerable. However, Boaz's only thoughts were to do what was right in the sight of the Lord. He was a man of integrity and dignity. The love of God in his heart dictated his response. He did only what was best for her.

God was watching. (He is always watching.) Boaz was greatly rewarded for his righteous choices. Following that night on the threshing floor, Boaz found the joys of sharing God's kind of love with Ruth. Their marriage union before the Lord was ordained by God. It became a vital part of the scarlet thread of salvation history.

3. God's kind of love is not concerned with the fear of man (what others may think). It only considers what is right. This is clear in the protective love Joseph showed Mary when he found out she was chosen by God to be with Child by the Holy Spirit. Joseph disregarded his own reputation and comfort to protect and care for Mary. Joseph teaches us that fear of what people think gives way to the sacrificial protection of those we are given to care for. Joseph did so without regard to what anybody might have said. He knew what a precious gift Mary was to him and treated her accordingly.

4. God's kind of love protects others from exposure to ridicule and criticism.

- It never exposes or uncovers those who may find themselves in vulnerable positions.
- It shields others from the assault of uncaring, harsh, evil words (or people).
- It quiets those who are in turmoil, fear or confusion. Then, it pursues the circumstances around the person in turmoil, doing what it can to change things.
- It speaks assurance to people who believe they are unworthy of God's love.
- It follows the pattern of Jesus (below), who destroyed both the threat and the fear the storm brought, by speaking the Word of God.

Mark 4:39 (NKJV)

"Then He arose and rebuked the wind, and said to the sea, "Peace, be still!" And the wind ceased and there was a great calm."

Your responsibility is to intervene personally, whenever love requires doing so. You may not always be able to change the situation. You will have the opportunity to change the outlook of the person involved in the situation, because he or she will know that someone genuinely cares enough to take action.

5. God's kind of love never lacks opportunities to display itself. It is always looking for them. It is proactive when possible, but reacts when necessary. This displays the love of Christ as it moves to change the situation.

6. God's kind of love never sits in the judgment seat. This is exclusively reserved for Christ. If we judge others, we invite judgment upon ourselves. Our carnal nature

sometimes forgets this principle. We too easily and too often fall into the trap of sitting in judgment toward others. God invites us to sit in a different place. It is at the table of fellowship and forgiveness. There, Jesus will be waiting to join you in showing love to those who may have sinned or made mistakes. Like each of us, they are to be offered grace.

Matthew 7:1-2 (NKJV)

"Judge not, that you be not judged. {2} For with what judgment you judge, you will be judged; and with the measure you use, it will be measured back to you."

Ephesians 2:8-9 (NKJV)

"For by grace you have been saved through faith, and that not of yourselves; it is the gift of God, {9} not of works, lest anyone should boast."

God's kind of love protects those for whom it is responsible, because it sees them as precious and beyond earthly value. It does this because this love in us sees with the perspective of Christ. It protects, encourages, honors, enriches, covers and empowers those who are discouraged and downcast. As Jesus said in Matthew 25:40b, *"...inasmuch as you did it to one of the least of these My brethren, you did it to Me."*

A Spiritual Act in a Carnal World

The conviction to protect those who are needy is an essential spiritual act in the midst of our carnal world. It is the essence of sacrificial love. It is the display of the pure light of the

Lord, shining ever brighter from within us to bathe the world in the hope of Jesus Christ.

Some years ago, I was teaching for a week in Hong Kong at a Chinese language Bible school. At the end of my final lesson (which happened to be about God's love), I told a story I had once heard. I do not know where it originated. Let me tell you the story; and then, I will tell you what followed. The story is about a blind girl selling apples in an airport.

> It was the end of the week and three businessmen were hurrying through the airport to catch their flight home. They were late and knowing the plane was about to leave, they began to run. As they ran through the terminal, one of them tripped over a young blind girl, who was selling apples at a table. As the man tripped, he upset the table. The table, chair, apples, and the girl were scattered in the mist of all the people making their way to their gates. The man who had tripped caught up with the other two men. As they continued to run toward the gate, he stopped and looked back. Then he called to his friends and said, "When you can, tell my wife I missed the plane and will be back home in the morning."
>
> He went back to where the young blind girl was sitting on the floor in the midst of all the spilled apples. She was crying and did not know what to do. Everyone was watching but no one was helping. The man stooped down, spoke gently to

her and picked up the table and chair. He helped her to sit down, and spoke gently to her not to worry. He told her he would pick up the apples and put those that were not damaged back where they had been. He discarded the apples that were damaged. He assured her that everything was back in order and gave her more than enough money to cover the price of the damaged apples. He comforted her and then departed, to go and exchange his ticket for a flight in the morning. He was satisfied that he had done the right thing to protect her from the consequences of being alone on the floor of that concourse.

As the man walked away, the young blind girl called out to him. He stopped and turned. "Yes, what is it?" he said. She thought for a moment and asked him this question. "Sir, are you Jesus?"[7]

The students were touched deeply by the message behind the story. It was silent and God was speaking. Finally, I prayed and ended the session. The students all filed out of the classroom, except for two young women, who came up to me from the back of the classroom, arm in arm. I had not noticed them before. Now, I was about to experience one of those humbling moments that only God's kind of love can bring. As they approached me, I suddenly realized that one of them was blind. As they stopped in front of me, the blind young woman said something like this. *"Thank you for the story you told us, and thank you for all you have given us*

---

[7] Source unknown.

this week. We understand the love of God so much better." If she had said to me, *"Sir, are you Jesus?"* it would not have affected me any more than what she said.

There is a world of hurting people waiting for you to be Jesus to them. Will you hurry on past them, or will you stop and wrap them in God's kind of love? This is more than a suggestion for your consideration. My prayer is that you receive it as a command from God for your obedient and immediate action.

Matthew 5:14-16 (NKJV)

"You are the light of the world. A city that is set on a hill cannot be hidden. {15} Nor do they light a lamp and put it under a basket, but on a lampstand, and it gives light to all who are in the house. {16} Let your light so shine before men, that they may see your good works and glorify your Father in heaven."

∽ 8 ∽

Love with a Trusting Heart.

1 Corinthians 13:7 (NKJV)
"believes all things,"

1 Corinthians 13:7 (NIV)
(Love) "...always trusts,"

This fictional story makes a great beginning to this chapter.

A man was hiking through the woods, when a heavy fog rolled in. He could barely see where his next step would take him. Soon he became disoriented and lost his way. Suddenly, he stepped off the edge of a steep embankment and began to fall. On the way down, he managed to grab onto a tree root that was sticking out of the edge of the embankment. There he hung, not knowing what was below him. It was too foggy to see anything at all and he was unable to climb back up.

He hung there until his arms began to ache. In desperation, he cried, *"Help! Is anybody up there? Help me, I am about to fall!"* After a minute or so, he heard a voice that said, *"Let go of the branch."*

When the man heard that, he asked, *"What did you say?"* The reply came back, *"Let go of the branch."* By this time, his arms ached so badly that he knew he could not hold on much longer. He was slowly losing his grip.

As he hung in the heavy fog, the hiker did not liking the idea of letting go of the only thing that secured him from whatever lay below. He said, *"Who is this?"* This time, the voice said, *"This is God. Let go of the branch."* The hiker thought about it for a moment. Then he shouted, *"Is anybody else up there?"* Now there was dead silence. Finally, unable to endure the pain in his arms any longer, he surrendered to his fate… He released his grip and fell the entire eighteen inches, until his feet hit the ground.[8]

There will be times when God will not explain to you why you must trust Him. Just do what He says. When doubts creep in, simply let go of them and obey. Remember that trust is a fragile thing. Once broken, it is not easily repaired. It reminds me of this old nursery rhyme.

> *"Humpty Dumpty sat on a wall.*
> *Humpty Dumpty had a great fall.*
> *All the king's horses and all the king's men,*
> *Couldn't put Humpty together again."*[9]

---

[8] Adapted from Michael P. Green, Illustrations for Biblical Preaching, Baker, Electronic Edition, Grand Rapids, 1989.

[9] Humpty Dumpty is a character in an English language nursery rhyme, originally a riddle. The rhyme has a Roud Folk Song Index number of 13026.(Wikipedia).

Do not be like Humpty Dumpty and let your trust in God fall down. Give it a sure and secure place in your heart.

Proverbs 3:5-6 (NKJV)

"Trust in the LORD with all your heart, And lean not on your own understanding; {6} In all your ways acknowledge Him, And He shall direct your paths."

Proverbs 30:5 (NKJV)

"Every word of God is pure; He is a shield to those who put their trust in Him."

Trust and Your Relationships

You will find many occasions when trust between you and someone else is challenged. At these times, you will have the opportunity to display the love of Christ, without any undue demands on the other person. However, in godly relationships between two or more people, trust is a reciprocal dynamic. It is an unspoken covenant.

If relationships are to be healthy and whole, they must be based on a covenant of trust. Otherwise, they are destined to hurt one or both, or if in a group, many. A large part of loving others is that you make the choice to trust them, as they do you. You believe the best in them. They believe the best in you. When the trust is broken, what you are left with are the remains of a chaotic fall into a "Humpty Dumpty" conclusion. When trust is broken, covenant is shattered. Then, the relationship is often beyond repair.

Knowing how fragile relationships can be should motivate you to pursue the facts before losing your trust in someone. This is why truthfulness and transparency work so well in relationships. These two qualities (or choices) leave no place for deception or misunderstanding. They flood light into situations and prevent you from losing trust for the wrong reasons. Relationships are precious and worth every effort to secure and protect.

My experience has taught me that trying to deceive or lie fails every time. It has been easier for me to be truthful and transparent. This protects me. It also keeps those in my relationships from misunderstandings or worse. (As the previous chapter taught, loving others *"always protects."*) Ask yourself how well you handle those things that tempt you to lose your trust in others. Do you react from within your feelings before taking the time to discover and uncover the facts? If so, this could be a wakeup call to ask the Holy Spirit to help your initial responses to be more patient and carefully measured.

Because the exercise of God's kind of love invites us to make a choice to trust, it will be helpful if you learn to approach your relationships with a sense of careful, wise discernment. Do your best to see what those you would trust are really made of. Usually, there is a place inside your heart where you cannot fool yourself. Far too often, our emotional need to belong darkens and stifles our sense of discernment. We fool ourselves by denying the truth. We become trapped, awaiting the hurt and disappointment that will inevitably fall upon us, because we blinded ourselves to what we have sensed. Have you been there? I have and know that it is not

God's will that our spirits are crushed under the weight of these situations.

Things that Kill Trust

We all carry within ourselves the potential to do things that kill trust between us and others. Below, is a list of common reasons why trust is violated and destroyed. There are certainly many reasons that do not appear on the list, but it is a good starting point with which to check ourselves.

1. Lying (and being lied to)

   I have placed lying at the top of the list because it is the quickest way to destroy trust. Once a lie is uncovered, it immediately generates negative feelings. It signals caution to the person or people to whom the lie was told. Their reactions are typically to draw back from their relationships or association with the liar. The result is that walls are built, and access to people's hearts is denied.

   How easily and often do you lie to people? Have you considered that even the smallest of lies is not acceptable behavior?

2. Irresponsible behavior

   Trust is killed quickly by irresponsible behavior, because it demonstrates a lack of value placed on the transaction or relationship. People are usually quick to discern true intentions. Just as quickly, they withdraw their trust.

How much value do you normally place on the need to fulfill your responsibilities? Do you give them priority over whatever might distract you from them?

3. Uncaring behavior

It is hard to separate uncaring and irresponsible behavior. They are like twins who are difficult to tell apart. In both cases, people quickly withdraw their trust. Uncaring behavior is perhaps more damaging, because of the message it sends to those it damages.

Consider those times when you hurt someone because you chose not to care. (We have all done this.) God's kind of love demands that you place the highest priority on consideration for the feelings of others. Do not pass by this thought too quickly. Think carefully about your vulnerability to uncaring behavior.

4. Attraction to worldly things (a worldly lifestyle)

Temptation is everywhere. You need to understand this. You also need to know how to resist it. Attraction to the things of the world will bring a powerful temptation to trust in yourself, instead of God. The antidote for this is to draw near to God as you resist the temptation. Here, again, is James' wisdom on drawing near to God.

James 4:7-8a (NKJV)

"Therefore submit to God. Resist the devil and he will flee from you. {8} Draw near to God and He will draw near to you..."

There is a story told about a rich old woman who lived at the top of a high hill. The left side of the driveway to her house was very close to the edge of a steep drop off. She was interviewing for a chauffer to drive her car. Three men applied and she had each one drive her car up the hill while she watched. The first man showed off his driving skills by getting within one foot of the steep drop off. He was very pleased with himself. The second man, trying to do better than the first, managed to drive six inches from the edge. He was even more pleased with himself than the first man was. Finally, the third applicant drove the car up the hill. All the way up, he ran over the plants and grass on the right side of the driveway. The first two men could not help but laugh at him… until that is, the woman hired the third, apparently careless driver. However, things are not always what they seem.

The woman explained to the first two men that, though they certainly knew how to drive close to the edge, she preferred to be in a car that never came anywhere near to it. The third man had stayed as far away from the edge as he could. He was never tempted to see how close to disaster he could get. This was the man she hired to be her driver.[10]

The first two men had killed her trust. They had done the wrong thing, even as they ridiculed the third man for doing what was right. Taking chances and disregarding

---

[10] Source unknown.

what is right will tempt you to lean on your own abilities and kill your trust in God.

Trusting God should be our model. It has many parallels to trusting other people. The primary difference is that God is perfect. He never miscalculates or makes mistakes. Therefore, He is worthy of our trust in every situation. We, however, will make mistakes. Sometimes, we may trust those who are untrustworthy. We may even let down others who trusted us. If we fail to be trustworthy and do not value it as an attribute of great worth, we will be like the two drivers who took chances at the edge of the driveway. Eventually, their disregard for a safe journey would have caused a disaster.

Practical Steps to a Trustworthy Heart

1. Imitate the Lord. Be as much like Him as you can be.

1 Corinthians 11:1 (NKJV)

"Imitate me, just as I also imitate Christ."

Though you certainly are not God, you can do your best to take on some of His attributes. Among these is (as humanly as possible) to be trustworthy. When we think of God, we label His trustworthiness as faithfulness. He is absolute in His faithfulness toward us. You will be the deciding factor on whether you are trustworthy and faithful. Nobody else can make this decision for you.

2. The second practical step is always to remind yourself to value your integrity above the other things that will tug at your heart. You must measure yourself by how important

being honestly Christ-like is to you. I have found it to be far more important to do the right thing than to be liked or to please people. Always check your words and actions to be sure they preserve your integrity and demonstrate that you can be trusted.

Integrity or trustworthiness is often a sacrificial choice. Being a person who can be trusted may cost you in the moment. If you fail to act with integrity, you will learn a painful lesson. Once having spent your integrity and trustworthiness, you will find there are no refunds. You cannot get it back. People will remember your failures long after they forget your successes. Therefore, in those times that call for you to be trustworthy, do the right thing. It will preserve your integrity. You will find that this will turn out to be a blessing for you and the others to whom you have stayed faithful.

3. Condition yourself, and therefore your heart, to see people as God sees them. Look with compassion on them. Honor your word to them because you care about them. Jesus was our model. He was motivated to heal and deliver the oppressed because He was filled with compassion.

4. This step to a trustworthy heart is related closely to seeing people as God sees them. To put this into proper perspective, consider that Jesus endured the cross because He esteemed others more highly than He esteemed Himself. Because of this, countless numbers of us would one day call Him Savior. He considered our eternities more precious than His own life and well-being. Most of us will never experience anything that approaches having to endure crucifixion, but Jesus gave us a pattern to

follow in which He considered our lives as a higher priority then His own.

Philippians 2:1-4 (NKJV)

"Therefore if there is any consolation in Christ, if any comfort of love, if any fellowship of the Spirit, if any affection and mercy, {2} fulfill my joy by being like-minded, having the same love, being of one accord, of one mind. {3} Let nothing be done through selfish ambition or conceit, but in lowliness of mind let each esteem others better than himself. {4} Let each of you look out not only for his own interests, but also for the interests of others."

In Philippians 2, the Apostle Paul gave us perhaps the most compelling and unfailingly practical step to becoming trustworthy. We are to humble ourselves and *"esteem others better"* than ourselves. This will motivate us to do the right things for others. This will cause them to call us trustworthy. When we choose to look upon others as better than ourselves, it does not mean we think less of ourselves. It simply means we have had compassion and chose to value the well-being of others above ourselves. This is the sacrificial course of action that defines God's kind of love.

Perhaps you have not been trustworthy in the past. I have something to add to that poem about Humpty Dumpty. It might have been true that *"all the king's horses and all the king's men couldn't put Humpty together again."* However, if this nursery rhyme was actually speaking of a believer's life, with all its physical and emotional ups and downs, it could be stated this way.

Humpty Believer sat on a wall.
Humpty Believer had a great fall.
All the king's horses and all the king's men,
Couldn't put Humpty together again.

In His grace and mercy, God stepped in.
Humpty's shattered life once more began,
As God put Humpty together again.

Humpty found himself whole,
He found Himself free.
He found Himself sitting on "Abba's"[11] knee.

Hope was restored and faith was renewed.
Humpty was saved. His Father proved true.

My Definition of Grace

Grace is all the unlimited ability and goodness of God, which is the pure expression of His limitless, unbounding love. It is just waiting for you. God releases it in your time of need. It need not be earned, nor can it be. It is what you could never do for yourself and only He can do for you. It is sufficient for any circumstance. It is most often expressed through one person to another.

---

[11] See Romans 8:15.

Love with a Hopeful Heart.

1 Corinthians 13:7b (NKJV)

(Love) "hopes all things,"

1 Corinthians 13:7 (NIV)

(Love) "...always hopes"

To hope is to have a confident expectation that the good things you desire will be realized. In the New Testament, hope is often closely related to faith and trust in the Lord. Their meanings are connected through the similarities of their Greek root words, *"elpis"*[12] and *"pistis."*[13] The early translators of the New Testament often rendered them interchangeably, as *"hope," "trust"* or *"faith."*

1 Thessalonians 2:19 (NKJV)

"For what is our hope, or joy, or crown of rejoicing? Is it not even you in the presence of our Lord Jesus Christ at His coming?"

---

[12] Strong's Number G1679.
[13] Strong's Number G4102.

Paul considered being part of the family of believers, forever with Christ, as the successful manifestation of his hopes. He knew that his confident expectations for eternity were not wishful thinking. They were a faith-filled look into the future, seeing what cannot be seen with natural eyes, and knowing what cannot be known with the natural mind. They were a spiritual exercise of his confident expectations. Therefore, we can begin to define hope as *the confident expectation that the promises of our loving God toward us, which we know and see in the spirit, will one day be realized.*

Those without Christ, whose hearts are hardened to the truth, have no hope of an eternally blessed future. Others may have been given untrue and misleading hopes for their eternities through false teaching. The only basis of hope is our relationship with Christ, through the New Covenant in His blood sacrifice. Ephesians 2:12 tells us that those without this relationship are *"strangers from the covenant of promise,"* which is given to us in the New Testament.

Ephesians 2:12 (NKJV)

"that at that time you were without Christ, being aliens from the commonwealth of Israel and strangers from the covenants of promise, having no hope and without God in the world."

As born-again believers, our hope is based on this *"covenant of promise."* Because of Christ's sacrifice, we have indisputable assurance of our eternal futures. I have established my own definition of hope. Here it is.

Hope is the confident expectation that the promises of God toward us will come to pass. We know this is true, because we have read them in the Word of God and see them in the spirit. Our confidence is based on the completely dependable assurance of the eternally unchanging covenant of promise, the New Covenant made through Christ's blood sacrifice.

Knowing what hope is helps you to have an attitude of expectation, as you await the faithfulness of God to make itself manifest. However, hope is more than just an attitude. It is far beyond simply wishful thinking. It is a decision to stand and wait for what is in your heart, even when there seems to be no apparent reason to do so. Hebrews 11:1 assures you that hope's power lies in its substance, which the Scriptures define as faith. When faith is strong in your heart, hope becomes a tangible tool for success. It is something solid upon which you can depend. You can cling to this valuable truth in times when natural circumstances seem to contradict your expectations.

Hebrews 11:1 (NKJV)

"Now faith is the substance of things hoped for, the evidence of things not seen."

When I fought my difficult fight with cancer, I had only my faith upon which to base my hope for healing. As time went by, I saw my faith rewarded with the outcome for which I had been hoping. It was a wonderful moment. I continue to praise the One in whom I had hoped. Jesus was, is and always will be my divine Healer. He is forever faithful. In the next chapter, you will read my celebration testimony of God's faithfulness. Hope turned into the accomplishment of faith. My faith became a strong reservoir of future hope for whatever might come. It was God's demonstration of His kind of love in action. He could not help Himself. It is part of His nature and His good pleasure. Praise His name forever!

I had watched the faithfulness of God prove the worth of my hope. I understood that, through my love relationship to Christ, He provided me with a combination of three eternally available, always effective, unfailing gifts - faith, hope and love. This was a profound confirmation to me at the time when I needed it most. I want to express the truth of what I learned to you with the simplicity of the International Children's Bible version of this truth.

1 Corinthians 13:13 (ICB)

"So these three things continue forever: faith, hope and love. And the greatest of these is love."

Faith, hope and love are so wrapped around each other that they form a strong, unbreakable lifeline for each of us, as we believe God. Because of this, you can hang onto your faith, hope and love, knowing that when your grip starts to slip, you will remain in God's grip. His hand never wearies. It never slips. It is completely dependable and always able.

God's grip is an amazing thing, because it is not always felt in those times when you desperately want to feel it. However, your hope does not depend on what you feel, but rather, who you know. When you know God as your heavenly Father, through His Son Jesus Christ, your hope finds its substance, which is your faith. That is why the message of 1 Corinthians 13:13 is so completely tied to Hebrews 11:1. Look once more at the message of this verse.

Hebrews 11:1 (NKJV)

"Now faith is the substance of things hoped for, the evidence of things not seen."

Though it may seem as if you are alone, you are not. God is always there and able to intervene with His promises and power. He never fails. As you read the following legend of a Native American boy entering manhood, allow its message to speak to you about God's faithful presence. He is your heavenly Father. Regardless of whether or not you see Him in your circumstances, He is always there watching over you. Here is the legend. The original source of this story is unknown to me. It was told to me by my good friend, Pastor Bill Michael.

> "There is a legend told of the Cherokee Indian youth's rite of Passage. His father takes him into the forest, blindfolds him and leaves him alone. He is required to sit on a stump the whole night and not remove the blindfold until the rays of the morning sun are shining through it. He cannot cry out for help to anyone. Once he survives the night, he is considered by his tribe to be a fully grown, fully responsible man of the tribe.
>
> The young Cherokee cannot tell the other boys of this experience, because each of them must come

into manhood on his own. As he sits on the stump in the dark forest, the boy is naturally terrified. He can hear all kinds of noises. Wild beasts must surely be all around him. Maybe even some person might come and do him harm. Though the wind blew the grass and earth, and shook his stump, he sat stoically, never removing the blindfold. This would be the only way he could become a man!

Finally, after a seemingly endless, horrific night, the sun appeared and he removed his blindfold. It was then that he discovered his father sitting on the stump next to him. Though the son never knew it or felt his presence, the father had been at watch the entire night, protecting his son from harm. We, too, are never alone.

Even when we do not know it, God is watching over us, sitting on the stump beside us. When trouble comes, all we have to do is reach out to Him. Just because you cannot see God, does not change the fact that He is there with you. Even in the darkest hours, He is watching. For we walk by faith, not by sight."

Practical Steps to Holding Fast to Hope in Christ

1. Persevere without doubting or wavering.

Like the young Cherokee boy, you may become fearful of the unknown, or blind to the circumstances around you. God's kind of love is always greater than your circumstances. He will never leave you unattended. He will be there to watch over you. Stay consistent in your hope because God is consistent in His loving faithfulness.

Hebrews 10:23 (NKJV)

"Let us hold fast the confession of our hope without wavering, for He who promised is faithful."

James 1:6-8 (NKJV)

"But let him ask in faith, with no doubting, for he who doubts is like a wave of the sea driven and tossed by the wind. {7} For let not that man suppose that he will receive anything from the Lord; {8} he is a double-minded man, unstable in all his ways."

2. Give a voice to your hopes when doubt begins to speak. Never give a voice to your doubts. Keep your doubts silent and they will have no life.

The key to seeing your hopes realized is twofold. First, according to the instructions in Hebrews 10:23, you must hold fast to your confession. Declare your faith and then, stick with it. Second, audibly announce the faithfulness of God to anyone who can hear (especially to your own ears). If necessary, make it a shout! As you do this, thank God for fulfilling your hopes. At that moment, it may be a declaration of thanksgiving, spoken ahead of what you hope to become reality in your life. Do not be swayed by any delay you may experience. Continue to speak of your hopes with thanksgiving. Never, ever, give any room in your heart, mind or mouth to speak words of doubt. Cast them down and shut them out. In Christ, with the help of

God and His love, you have the ability and strength to do so. Just keep giving voice to your hopes. God is faithful. His kind of love never fails.

Philippians 4:5b-7 (NKJV)

"...The Lord is at hand. {6} Be anxious for nothing, but in everything by prayer and supplication, with thanksgiving, let your requests be made known to God; {7} and the peace of God, which surpasses all understanding, will guard your hearts and minds through Christ Jesus."

2 Corinthians 10:5 (NKJV)

"casting down arguments and every high thing that exalts itself against the knowledge of God, bringing every thought into captivity to the obedience of Christ,"

You have read of the power in persevering and speaking words of hope. As a believer, you have faith, hope and love, working together to insulate you from your doubts and unbelief. The battleground for your fight, to see your hopes become real, is your mind. This brings us to our third practical step for being strategic in the battleground and winning your victory within it.

3. Focus your thinking on virtuous and praiseworthy things.

Paul continued to instruct the Philippian church on how to hold fast to their hopes with these words, which follow. As you read them, notice that everything Paul says to meditate upon is positive and uplifting. These are instructions filled with God's kind of love and His wisdom for the ages. Take particular notice of *"whatever things are pure."* Only pure things are filled with God's kind of love and wisdom. They have nothing evil or compromising mixed in them that would pollute you.

> *Philippians 4:8 (NKJV)*
>
> *"Finally, brethren,*
> *whatever things are true,*
> *whatever things are noble,*
> *whatever things are just,*
> *whatever things are pure,*
> *whatever things are lovely,*
> *whatever things are of good report,*
> *if there is any virtue*
> *and if there is anything praiseworthy;*
> *meditate on these things."*

The original Greek word for *"meditate"* is *"logizomai."* This word originally meant, *"To take an inventory of your thoughts."*[14] As the chapter concludes, I invite you to take an inventory of your thoughts concerning the three practical steps you have been given to enable you to hold fast to your hope in Christ. Here they are again.

1. Persevere without doubting or wavering.

2. Give a voice to your hopes when doubt begins to speak.

3. Focus your thinking on virtuous and praiseworthy things.

---

[14] Strong's Number 3049.

Love with an Enduring Heart.

1 Corinthians 13:7 (NLT)

(Love) "...endures through every circumstance."

1 Corinthians 13:7b (NIV)

(Love) "...always perseveres."

In the year 2001, the cancer was finally gone from my body. The mighty, loving hand of my forever-faithful God had healed me. I was filled with thanksgiving and gratefulness. I had endured, but more importantly, God had endured with me. He never left me. He was always there.

Matthew 28:20b (NKJV)

"...and lo, I am with you always..."

Following the miraculous outcome of my struggle with cancer, I wrote a poem. It was a celebration of my heartfelt thanksgiving to God. Because of His presence, even though I had been fighting an apparent death sentence, I never gave in, gave up or gave out! I had endured so much, but I just kept believing God was who He said He was, and would do what His Word said He would do. I never allowed doubt to enter, even in the most painful and difficult times. I had determined, at the first report that I would endure to the final report. I knew that the final report would justify my determination to endure without wavering… and it did.

What follows is my declaration of thanksgiving to God. Please let it speak to your heart. You may be going through what seems like a situation without any apparent hope. If not you, perhaps there is someone else you know who is in that difficult place in life. We will all find ourselves there at some point. I heartily recommend you place a copy of *"Not Moved"* somewhere you can readily refer to it. When a time to endure without wavering becomes critically important to you or someone else, share it. Recite it aloud. Declare it! Tell it to your circumstances. Most importantly, keep telling it to yourself until the time of endurance passes and your determination to believe God takes you to your victory.

NOT MOVED

Not moved by what I see...
  Not moved by what I hear.

Not moved by what I feel...
  Not moved by what I fear.

Though troubles may approach me...
  Though rumors may abound.

Though others may reproach me...
  I will reject that sound.

Though weakness may encroach...
  on my once abundant strength.

Though sickness comes and cloaks me...

In Christ I will remain.
Not moved by what attacks me...
Not moved by what I lack.

Not moved by who deserts me...
Not moved by who turns back.

Jesus is my Master... My Lord, my Strength, my Shield.
Though others may persuade me... To Him alone I yield.

I live for Him with confidence... In Spirit I am filled.
I live for Him with faithfulness... His kingdom I will build.

Not moved by what I see...
Not moved by what I hear.

Not moved by what I feel...
Not moved by what I fear.

Just moved by my Lord Jesus...
And moved by my own zeal.

Just moved by grace and mercy...
My life in Him is real!

Selah

Please take the time to read my celebration poem once again. Go ahead. Do it a second time. Meditate on it as you read. It is a testimony to the faithfulness of God. I know God will speak to you from within its declarations of endurance and faith. For many years, those to whom I pastored, mentored or ministered have heard my favorite saying about the names of God. It originally came from my dear friend Jide Olutamayin, who was an elder in my church in Fiji. It goes something like this. *"My wife has three names. Her first name is Nancy. Her middle name is Marie. Her last name is Abramson. She is Nancy Marie Abramson."* Then I would ask, *"Do you know what God's first, middle and last names are?"* This usually confuses the people to whom I ask the question. The answer becomes clear and the revelation is always powerful when I answer the question. Here is my answer.

> *"God's first name is "Faithful."*
> *His middle name is "Faithful."*
> *His last name is "Faithful."*
> *His complete name (and perhaps the most important one He has) is "Faithful Faithful Faithful!""*

It would be appropriate at this point to relate the connection between God's faithfulness, His kind of love, and His grace and mercy. This connection is the glue that holds together the Christian life, our liberty in Christ and the ability to endure the battle, until our *"Faithful Faithful Faithful"* God moves and the victory is ours. The thing that continually kept me standing in faith and hope during my battle with cancer was the Lord's grace and mercy. I have concluded that what moved God to provide His grace to heal me was His unfailing, completely faithful love. I endured because I chose to welcome my *"Faithful Faithful Faithful"* God to firmly and continually abide in my heart. God's kind of love never fails. Once again, I refer you to the message in 1 Corinthians 13:8. This time, I have also provided a translation from the Chinese Bible.

1 Corinthians 13:8a (NKJV)

"Love never fails..."

1 Corinthians 13:8a (Chinese Translation)

"Love is eternal..."

Put both translations together and you have a statement of fact, by which you can endure all things. I have paraphrased it this simple way.

God's kind of love is forever faithful and unfailing.

This paraphrase is a simple statement of an incredibly profound truth. You can place your trust in Him, knowing He is always there in your times of need. That is how your love *"endures all things."*

ಆಶ 11 ಆಶ

The Picture is Incomplete.

Take another look at the Apostle Paul's description of all the characteristics of *"agape"* or God's kind of love. This can become your checklist for progressively become more like Christ. How would you score yourself right now?

1 Corinthians 13:4-7 (NIV)

"Love is patient, love is kind. It does not envy, it does not boast, it is not proud. {5} It is not rude, it is not self-seeking, it is not easily angered, it keeps no record of wrongs. {6} Love does not delight in evil but rejoices with the truth. {7} It always protects, always trusts, always hopes, always perseveres."

As comprehensive as this checklist is, there is still more to God's kind of love than this list has given us. Now, let us journey deeper into the boundless depths of God's kind of love. We will do this by seeing what we can glean from the Lord's own words and the subsequent writings of His disciples. You might want to stop, review, and reflect what you have read so far. Then, as you continue, ask the Holy Spirit to melt your heart and transform any part of your thinking that still requires that it be renewed to match how Jesus thought, acted and loved during His time on earth. He is the model we seek to emulate. It is His good pleasure, by His Spirit, to help us do this.

There is an overwhelming body of biblical instruction concerning the Lord's expectations for our attitudes and actions toward others. Much of it comes from Jesus, Himself. Some of the things He said about His kind of love will help us gain practical insight into the value of it for ourselves. Below, are four principles of Jesus' kind of love that I have taken from Jesus' own words. They will help you define how you ought to live, so that you will influence those around you in positive, uplifting ways.

1. God's kind of love displays itself in you, as you obediently demonstrate it toward others.

   Obedience to keep the Lord's commands concerning love demonstrates two things. First, loving as God loves proves you are committed to honoring Him and His commandment to love. Second, loving as God loves proves you are His disciple.

   Matthew 22:37-39 (NKJV)

   "Jesus said to him, "'You shall love the LORD your God with all your heart, with all your soul, and with all your mind.' {38} This is the first and great commandment. {39} And the second is like it: 'You shall love your neighbor as yourself.'"[15]

---

[15] Jesus quoted portions of Leviticus 19:18, thus validating this principle for the ages.

John 13:34b-35 (NKJV)

"...as I have loved you, that you also love one another. {35} By this all will know that you are My disciples, if you have love for one another."

John 14:15 (NKJV)

"If you love Me, keep My commandments."

As you can see, obedience is not optional. If you love Jesus, He expects, and indeed, commands that you love others as you love Him. Make the personal choice to become someone who is a living testimony to God's kind of love. Prove it by your obedience. Then, go beyond obedience and genuinely care. Here are a few more examples of Jesus' teaching on this subject.

John 14:21 (NKJV)

"He who has My commandments and keeps them, it is he who loves Me. And he who loves Me will be loved by My Father, and I will love him and manifest Myself to him."

John 14:23-24 (NKJV)

"Jesus answered and said to him, "If anyone loves Me, he will keep My word; and My Father will love him, and We will come to him and make Our home with him. {24} He who does not love Me does not keep My words; and the word which you hear is not Mine but the Father's who sent Me."

John 15:10 (NKJV)

"If you keep My commandments, you will abide in My love, just as I have kept My Father's commandments and abide in His love."

2. God's kind of love proves itself by your selfless sacrifice.

John 15:13 (NKJV)

"Greater love has no one than this, than to lay down one's life for his friends."

John 15:13 records Jesus making a statement that has two distinct, but related messages. First, His words spoke in a prophetic sense to His disciples about His coming crucifixion. On the cross, He would become sin for us, so we might become the righteousness of God in Him. He would pay the debt we owed, so we did not have to pay it ourselves. The crucifixion would become history's singular act of divine sacrifice. Nothing else will ever compare to it. Second, His words in this verse provide a principle for the ages. If you are His disciple, He does not ask you to be nailed to His cross. That would make what He did of no effect. He asks you to embrace the principle of sacrifice that inherently defines His kind of love, as you selflessly claim it in your love for others. This will manifest itself daily if you give it the opportunity to do so.

Luke 9:23 (NKJV)

"Then He said to them all, "If anyone desires to come after Me, let him deny himself, and take up his cross daily, and follow Me.""

3. God's kind of love proves itself by imitating the Father.

John 17:26 (NKJV)

"And I have declared to them Your name, and will declare it, that the love with which You loved Me may be in them, and I in them."

I am reasonably sure that you have heard the timeworn saying that *"imitation is the sincerest form of flattery."*[16] I suppose this is because it contains a truth that passed the test of time. If this saying is true, then it makes sense that whomever you imitate, you flatter and honor. You choose to emulate those people in whom you find value in what their lives demonstrate and teach. Consider your daily activities. What are you doing that demonstrates who you have chosen to imitate? We know that the Apostle Paul entreats us to imitate him just as he imitated Christ (1 Corinthians 11:1). Look carefully at my paraphrase.

Reproduce, in you, the love of God that you find in Me.

4. God's kind of love proves itself in the believer's ministry.

I have just suggested that the imitation of God's kind of love is of the greatest flattery to Him. Therefore, it is reasonable to suggest that God's kind of love in you would lead to actions that prove it to be one of your primary characteristics. The Lord asked Peter to imitate Him in Peter's future life and ministry. This imitation became a scriptural model of love for us to demonstrate.

---

[16] Charles Caleb Colten (1780-1832) English sportsman, writer, "LaCon," Volume I (1825).

Jesus approached this subject with Peter. It was a challenge, a cause and effect argument. It was conditional on Peter's sacrifice and obedience.

John 21:15-17 (NKJV)

"So when they had eaten breakfast, Jesus said to Simon Peter, "Simon, son of Jonah, do you love Me more than these?" He said to Him, "Yes, Lord; You know that I love You." He said to him, "Feed My lambs." {16} He said to him again a second time, "Simon, son of Jonah, do you love Me?" He said to Him, "Yes, Lord; You know that I love You." He said to him, "Tend My sheep." {17} He said to him the third time, "Simon, son of Jonah, do you love Me?" Peter was grieved because He said to him the third time, "Do you love Me?" And he said to Him, "Lord, You know all things; You know that I love You." Jesus said to him, "Feed My sheep.""

Three times, Peter replied to Jesus, saying, *"You know I "phileo"*[17] *You."* The original Greek language tells us Peter was actually saying, *"You know I am 'fond' of you."* Peter's reply conveyed affection for Jesus. It fell short of saying he had God's kind of *"agape"* love toward Jesus. Nevertheless, the Lord accepted Peter's words because that was all Peter had to offer. Jesus knew that Peter's *"phileo"* would soon grow into genuine, fully committed *"agape."* Peter's coming years to come would demonstrate this. One day, Peter would be crucified for his *"agape"* of Jesus.

---

[17] Strong's Number G5368.

Our Obligation as Believers

Romans 13:8-10 (NKJV)

"Owe no one anything except to love one another, for he who loves another has fulfilled the law. {9} For the commandments, "You shall not commit adultery You shall not murder, You shall not steal, You shall not bear false witness, You shall not covet" and if there is any other commandment, are all summed up in this saying, namely, "You shall love your neighbor as yourself." {10} Love does no harm to a neighbor; therefore love is the fulfillment of the law."

Galatians 5:13-14 (NKJV)

"For you, brethren, have been called to liberty; only do not use liberty as an opportunity for the flesh, but through love serve one another. {14} For all the law is fulfilled in one word, even in this: "You shall love your neighbor as yourself.""

Paul provided this excellent set of obligations to the Roman and Galatian Christians (and to us). They were living in societies that had distinctly opposite moralities from what Paul laid down with these sets of instructions. The Holy Spirit has preserved them as cannon for us, so we may understand the will of the Father. This is not a complete list of our Christian obligations. We know the greatest commandment is to love the Lord with all our hearts, strength and mind. We also know that loving our neighbor as ourselves guarantees we will not deny any of our love obligations. They are all wrapped around loving others, as we would want to be loved. As Paul put it, we should owe nothing to one another except to love as God loves. Should we succeed in doing so, everything else will fall into place. Then, the picture will be closer to complete.

೧ೀ 12 ೧ೀ

Up Close and Personal

I will begin this chapter with a narrative from my book, "Just a Little Bit More - The Heart of a Mentor." In it wrote about a special moment in my life and ministry that was uniquely given by God, and I thought could never be repeated. Here is the narrative.

> "It was the year following my recovery from cancer (2001). We had left New York City and gone back to Florida. I had been away from Fiji for almost three years. Quite unexpectedly, I received an invitation to return and spend about six weeks ministering in Fiji. One of the high points of the trip would be a whirlwind journey around Fiji visiting the church-planting graduates of our ministry training center, which was called the School of Urban Missions. One of the people we would visit was Sakiusa Nasici (Everyone at our school called him "Saki."). He had planted a church in the mountains of Northern Viti Levu.[18] It was in a remote village community of gold mine workers.

---

[18] Viti Levu is the Fijian name for the primary island in the nation of Fij.

We arrived there for an evening service. Pastor Saki was in tears just to see us again. After the people had gathered, Nancy and I were ushered out to the yard behind his house. Saki had erected a series of poles made from local trees, which held a canopy of corrugated iron. There were no sides to this structure but it served as a very nice church. Electric lights hanging from bare wires illuminated the area. At the front was a pulpit constructed from some rough looking wood. Behind the pulpit sat two overstuffed chairs that had been brought from Saki's house for Nancy and me to sit in. Perhaps seventy-five people had gathered, and were sitting on the ground awaiting our arrival. They were almost all new converts. Saki had brought most of them to the Lord. They were ready for church!

After the congregation had worshiped and prayed, Saki introduced us. It took him about twenty minutes to tell the congregation how much we had meant to him, and how his time with us had changed him forever. He finally turned to Nancy and me, sitting in our overstuffed chairs. The few words He spoke to us carried more impact than all he could have said, had he stood there for hours on end. The words he spoke will ring in my heart forever. He simply said, *"Pastor Bob and Sister Nancy, I want to introduce you to your spiritual grandchildren."*[19]

---

[19] Dr. Bob Abramson, <u>Just a Little Bit More</u>, Alphabet Resources, © 2008, P.91.

As I said, I did not think this heart-rending experience would ever be repeated. It touched my heart so deeply that it is burned into my life forever. Pastor Ralph Hagemire has said, *"God is an also God."* He simply meant God can do two things at once, or He can repeat a blessing. To my surprise, He has repeated the blessing from Pastor Saki and his people, who he called, our *"spiritual grandchildren."* I had another heart-rending experience, just like this first one, the day before I wrote this. I could not wait to include it in the book. It is another one of those moments, in which God touched Nancy and me with His amazing kind of love. Here is the story of how it happened.

> We had encouraged one of our "spiritual daughters," whose name is Pastor Heaven Hsiao, to plant a Chinese-speaking church in Brooklyn, New York. The name of the church is Living Streams Christian Church. Its name reflects its character. It has become a wonderful family of winners and champions, full of life for Jesus. (I tell them that every chance I get.) Nancy and I had helped train and equip Pastor Heaven, but it was God at work in her, who was bringing such fruitful results to her church planting efforts.
>
> Pastor Heaven was determined to establish and grow a church of people who were new in the faith. She has done such a marvelous job, faithfully fulfilling God's call to do so. Each of the past two years, Nancy and I have gone with the church on a weekend retreat in April. It has been held in a beautiful retreat center in rural New Jersey. As we

did in the first year, Nancy and I taught the church each day of the retreat. Our subject for this year's set of meetings was, "The Christian Life - Truth and Love." I now realize that this was no coincidence. God used this time with His people to take me to places in His kind of love that I had never been. He indeed, is an *"also God."*

At the finish of the final session of the retreat, in the midst of a celebration of joy for what God had done, the people began to pray for Nancy and me. They called us "Baba Musha" and "Mama Musha."[20] These words roughly translate into "grandfather pastor" and "grandmother pastor." The people of the church told us we would always be their "spiritual grandparents."

It was a moment that caused all of our hearts to melt. Nancy and I were filled completely with emotions I cannot describe. It felt like a repeat of what happened years earlier, at Pastor Saki's church in that Fijian gold mining community. Now, twelve years later, God gave Nancy and me this unexpected, refreshing gift. It was worth more than words can express. It was worth more than all the gold that could come out of that mine in Fiji. It was priceless, precious and eternally ours. In a previous chapter, I included the Chinese equivalent of 1 Corinthians 13:8a. It speaks to what you have just read.

---

[20] The phonetic equivalent of Mandarin Chinese.

1 Corinthians 13:8a (Chinese Translation)

"Love is eternal..."

When you add these two experiences to the one I told you of, on my final night in Malaysia, praying for Johnny,[21] you have the heart of my message to you. In these three special moments, God has given Nancy and me an up close and personal glimpse of what it will be like when we all get around the throne of God. There will be so much of God's kind of love that it will cause us to worship joyfully and forever. We will do so on streets paved with gold that no person ever had to labor to extract from a mine. I sometimes wonder if the Lord will allow Nancy and me to have one more glorious experience like these three, about which you have read. I believe God wants to bless you with an equally significant experience. It will come as you give His kind of love to people - from your heart to theirs... up close and personal!

I have a few thoughts about what can be learned from these two stories of the two churches that called us their "spiritual grandparents."

1. Eternal blessings are carried in the power of words. Some of your best rewards will come from what you say to others, as you express your *"agape"* love.

2. The pattern of loving, as God loves, repeats itself through the words of others who have been receiving His kind of love from your words.

---

[21] Please take the time to return to Page 13 and read the story of Johnny once more.

3. There is incredible power in a name. We have the example in biblical times of people like Jacob, whose name God changed to Israel. With his name change came a significant change in his identity. It also brought a significant change in Jacob's position among his people. When the people of Living Streams Christian Church spoke the name "Baba Musha" over me, I realized what I meant to them, and what the name meant to me. This also led me to see why, a few years earlier, God had ended my season as the pastor of a wonderful church in New York City. He had a call on me that required my surrendering to His plan. It had become time to spread my wings and move ahead in God's plan for my life. In my present season, I am called to function as a father-like mentor across many time zones and into many lives. This motivates me to do the things that I know it is my time to do. I will be a father-like influence to pastors, and if my heart shows enough through my words and actions, I even might have the blessing of again being called, "Baba Musha" by somebody.

4. Every so often, we need a reality check to help balance our perspectives on life. I go through this each time I am challenged about God's kind of love, through the way I communicate with others. These times are offered to all of us by God. They provide those teachable moments we all need to help us to reflect on the condition of our hearts. If you are having trouble with a judgmental or hardened heart toward others, let yourself surrender to God's kind of love. When you do this, the hearts of others will surrender to you.

Love always begins with a choice.

God's kind of love gives us its strength when it begins with a choice. If it begins with an emotion, it has a shaky start. However, if it starts with a choice to be Christ-like in its attitudes, it can then build on additional correct choices. The emotions will follow, and that is good, because when the emotions are built on correct choices, they will be genuinely filled with God's grace. They will result in blessings.

Love always requires patience and the willingness to sacrifice self-serving motives. There is always God's kind of love awaiting your faith in Him and willingness to act according to His will. Do this until the love you need, and are able to provide to others, becomes a reality. Jesus is our example. His story is our model. It is called the Gospels.

There is one more story to tell. It is about my beginnings in ministry. In those early years, I had been well schooled in the hands-on techniques of pastoring, by my first mentor, Pastor Michael Davis. I had been working diligently to earn my theological degrees. I seemed to know the right things to say and do when I counseled or prayed for people. I was becoming a fairly competent preacher. My performance at the end of my sermons was more than adequate. I knew all the bells and whistles about altar ministry. I had arrived… or so I thought. God knew better. I was about to learn what He knew. I will tell you about it in the next chapter.

෴ 13 ෴

His Presence Transforms the Heart.

God's kind of love has been a commandment to God's people for thousands of years. Today, it remains as the core principle of Christian life. It will remain so until Jesus returns. Then, God's people will not need to be commanded to love. We will all be overwhelmed with love's presence among us. It will permeate our eternal existence. Until then, we have the Scriptures to remind us to *"love one another."*

1 John 4:21 (NKJV)

"And this commandment we have from Him: that he who loves God must love his brother also."

2 John 1:5-6 (NKJV)

"And now I plead with you, lady, not as though I wrote a new commandment to you, but that which we have had from the beginning: that we love one another. This is love, that we walk according to His commandments. This is the commandment, that as you have heard from the beginning, you should walk in it."

As we walk in love, there will be those unique, sometimes unexpected and always very special moments, when God transforms our hearts. This transformation requires three conditions, working together, to make it possible. These are (1) God's timing, (2) His voice, and (3) our willingness to receive what He says. I would like to share one of these rare and special moments in my life.

On the Back of the Platform

During my early years of serving God, I pastored a single adult ministry at Trinity Church International. We had services on Friday evenings. On one particular Friday, my wife Nancy and I were in the church sanctuary preparing for the evening service. No one else had yet arrived. We began praying for the service. What happened that evening was one of those moments that is vividly etched in my memory. It never seems to fade. Here is the story of what happened.

> I was a couple feet from the back wall on the left side of the platform. As was my custom, I was facing toward the wall, praying for the evening's service. Suddenly, I felt the deep, overwhelming presence of God. It was so heavy that I could hardly stand and continue to pray. The Holy Spirit began to speak to me. I cannot say it was an audible voice, but I clearly heard within my heart a command from Him that took me by surprise. It was a command from which I have never retreated. He wrote these words on my heart.
>
> *"Never preach to My people or pray for them until you find it in your heart to love them with My kind of love!"*

I was smitten with conviction and sorrow. I realized how hardened my heart had been. I could only sink to my knees and weep. I was found out! The Holy Spirit's message was simple. It was redemptive. It was delivered with love. His words revealed to me that I was filled with potential, with which I could achieve my destiny. I had been a performer, but God wanted me to be a lover. From now on, it would be God's kind of love or nothing… and nothing was not an option! In that moment, I was forever changed. There would be no turning back. I was a man on a mission. I would put on the garment of bond service to God. I would let my light shine with His kind of love.

This encounter with the Holy Spirit at the back of that altar happened many years ago. Yet, the memory of God's words penetrating my heart is as fresh as the day He spoke them to me. His words struck me like lightning, with a million Holy Spirit volts released into my heart. I am grateful that God did not leave me in the prideful, arrogant and ignorant place I was in at the time. I realized that I had misunderstood ministry. I thought it to be all about performance, not love. Though I am sure I fail at times, I have tried my best since then, to let the compassion of God's kind of love define my ministry these many years. My desire is that I will be known for having a compassionate heart, when all I have taught, preached or counseled is long forgotten.

I hope this story of the Holy Spirit speaking to me on the back of the platform will touch your heart as much as God touched mine when it happened. Please take the time to reflect on your life and the influence God's compassionate love could have on those to whom you will minister and for whom you will care. My story illustrates the foundational point of this book. God's kind of love is transformational. It is a powerful blessing to be received and shared.

Transformational Love

The great New Testament example of transformation is Saul of Tarsus. Acts, Chapter 26 records the testimony of his transformation, as he relates it to King Agrippa. It started with this question, *"Who are You Lord?"* Jesus answered Saul and so began his transformation into the great hero of the faith we know as the Apostle Paul. Here is Paul's testimony of this encounter with Jesus.

Acts 26:15-16 (NKJV)

"So I said, 'Who are You, Lord?' And He said, 'I am Jesus, whom you are persecuting. {16} But rise and stand on your feet; for I have appeared to you for this purpose, to make you a minister and a witness both of the things which you have seen and of the things which I will yet reveal to you.'"[22]

The Lord Jesus revealed to Saul the purpose for Saul's life. It transformed Saul forever. Later, as the Apostle Paul, he wrote to the Philippians. His instructions in his letter centered on the love he had learned from Jesus. Earlier, I quoted Philippians 2:1-4. Let us look at these Scriptures again.

---

[22] The original account is in Acts 9:1-9.

"Therefore if there is any consolation in Christ, if any comfort of love, if any fellowship of the Spirit, if any affection and mercy, {2} fulfill my joy by being like-minded, having the same love, being of one accord, of one mind. {3} Let nothing be done through selfish ambition or conceit, but in lowliness of mind let each esteem others better than himself. {4} Let each of you look out not only for his own interests, but also for the interests of others."

This passage of Scripture describes the process in which the transforming power of God's kind of love springs into action. From it, we may extract three timeless, highly descriptive foundations for this process. Each of them begins with an *"if."* This makes the outcomes conditional on our willingness to display these foundations to others. As you read, let the sum of their individual parts speak to you. These parts are (1) *"consolation and comfort,"* (2) *"fellowship"* and (3) *"affection and mercy."* Add these parts together with daily worship of God, and they form the pattern for successful Christian living - love in action.

1. *"Therefore, if there is any consolation in Christ, if any comfort of love,"*

   The original Greek words Paul used for *"consolation"* is *"paraklesis,"*[23] and for *"comfort"* is *"paramuthion."*[24] They are essentially synonymous. They both speak of

---

[23] Strong's Number G3874.
[24] Strong's Number G3890.

God's comfort through Christ and His love. The implication is that if these first two conditions are present in the believer's interaction with others; and the other two "*ifs* accompany them, then unity will follow. (It is illuminating to note that the Greek word with which Jesus referred to the Holy Spirit as "*Comforter*" (KJV) is "*Parakletos.*" Other translations refer to Him as our "*Helper*" or "*Counselor.*"[25])

2. "*...if any fellowship of the Spirit,*"

The Apostle Paul was intimately aware of the difference between carnal living and living in the Spirit. (A reading of the Romans, Chapter 8 will confirm how intensely Paul felt about this subject.) When we add this element of "*fellowship in the Spirit*" to the comfort we enjoy through Christ and His love, it leads us to the third part of this pattern for successful Christian living.

3. "*...if any affection and mercy,*"

It is striking that this third part gets its meaning from two Greek words. The first, "*splagchnon,*"[26] can be translated literally as, "*bowels*" or "*innermost parts.*" It speaks of affectionate feelings that emanate from the deepest, inward parts of our bodies. The second, "*oiktirmos,*"[27] speaks of compassion and mercy. Together, they define the character of a follower of Christ. The Lord's desire is that "*affection and mercy*" come out from deep within us to make a difference all around us.

---

[25] "*Helper*" - NKJV, GWT, ICB; "*Counselor*" - NLT, NIV.
[26] Strong's G4698.
[27] Strong's G3628.

The quality of the fellowship with our brothers and sisters in Christ depends on whether our hearts are transformed and are a reflection of the Word of God.

- We are to place a priority on providing each other with God's kind of comfort and love, in ways that can only come through us.
- We are to walk consistently and peaceably with each other, as we walk with God.
- We are to give God's compassionate mercy to each other.

Look again at Philippians 2:3-4. As they complete Paul's thoughts, which began in Verses 1 and 2, they seem to offer both instructions in righteous action and a warning to us.

> *{3} "Let nothing be done through selfish ambition or conceit, but in lowliness of mind let each esteem others better than himself. {4} Let each of you look out not only for his own interests, but also for the interests of others."*

These two verses warn us not to allow our natural, carnal tendencies to influence or control our interactions with others. Paul cautions us to beware of selfish ambitions and prideful thinking. Then, He provides the contrast, which is to consider the well-being of others to be of higher importance than our own well-being. Finally, Paul instructs us not to be self-centered and selfish. It is good to be concerned for ourselves, as we should be, but we are not to neglect giving a high regard to the interests of others.

Redemption, though instant, invites us into a process of transformation that lasts for a lifetime. We call this sanctification. It means we are changing to become more like Jesus, on a daily basis, until we finally enter into eternity in the presence of God. Learning to love as God does is the foundation of this transformation. This love is displayed in our actions and words, which come from a softened and renewed heart. When there is an abundance of His kind of love, we become demonstrations of its power and potential.

Luke 6:45 (NKJV)

"A good man out of the good treasure of his heart brings forth good; and an evil man out of the evil treasure of his heart brings forth evil. For out of the abundance of the heart his mouth speaks."

Below, is my paraphrase of Luke 6:45, as it speaks to the issues of His transforming presence in our hearts.

The love God places in a person's heart is a gift of potential richness. As we embrace and develop it into an abundance of invaluable life-giving treasure, our words will bring forth good, comforting and edifying results. For out of the abundance of our hearts, our mouths will give testimony to the transforming power of God.

❦ 14 ❦

The Journey Continues.

I have shared a great deal of what is in my heart concerning God's kind of love. In the preface, I began with this.

> "I am convinced that God's kind of love is the essence of His nature. Therefore, it is so vast and multifaceted that it is beyond any earthly attempt to record it fully in a book. Nevertheless, I believe that what follows can be your open door to the same kind of life's journey I am taking. With all its unexpected turns, my life is a walk on a path of discovery about who God is and what His love means to me... let your life's journey center on discovering the same."

One of my favorite (and often used) Scriptures is Proverbs 4:18. I think this is because it reflects my own journey to discover as much about God's kind of love as I can. I am inviting you to read this verse and consider how it might motivate you to do as I have done - to look more deeply into your relationship with God and His kind of love. I admit that I have not been as successful at this as I would like, but it is the path of my destiny. I am grateful to the Lord that He has called me to travel it. I am never alone on it. He is always with me. I am never in the dark. He lights my way more brightly, day by day. That is His promise. He will be there for you, too. It begins for each of us with walking the path of righteousness. The Amplified Bible Paraphrase of Proverbs 4:18 will help you see the divinely designed value of this path, upon which we are given to walk. It leads us to a brighter understanding of God's love.

Proverbs 4:18 (AMP)

"But the path of the [uncompromisingly] just and righteous is like the light of dawn, that shines more and more (brighter and clearer) until [it reaches its full strength and glory in] the perfect day [to be prepared]."

God is Love.

In the first chapter, I quoted 1 John 4:8 and 4:16, in which the Apostle John tells us that *"God is love."* This is a perfectly clear, concise statement of God's identity. Love is who God is. Love reflects what He has done in the past. It is seen in what He is doing today. It will be seen in what He will do in the future. God is the perfect model of love. Knowing Him, gives you a way to judge whether what is called love is truly God's kind of love. Only a reflection of His character and actions is love. Nothing else is truly love. In Acts, Chapter 9, when Saul of Tarsus asked Jesus who He was, the Lord answered. It was the beginning of Saul's life-long discovery process. Saul found out that, in all Jesus' splendor and majesty, His core identity is the essence of love. Saul (now Paul) summed it up in 1 Corinthians 13:2, as He wrote, without love *"I am nothing."*

Knowing that Christ's essence is love allows us to understand why He behaves toward us as He does. God's kind of love is the manifestation of His grace, in its fullest measure.

God loved you before you loved Him. His love for you is not based on your behavior, thoughts, outward appearance, strengths, shortcomings or mistakes. God loves you just the way you are. The purpose of Jesus' loving sacrifice on the cross was to make a way for you to have access to God, so you can love Him both now and throughout eternity. When you accept Jesus as your Lord and Savior, nothing can separate you from His love. I have chosen the International Children's Bible to illustrate this, because of its simplicity.

Romans 8:35, 37-39 (ICB)

"Can anything separate us from the love Christ has for us? Can troubles or problems or sufferings? If we have no food or clothes, if we are in danger, or even if death comes--can any of these things separate us from Christ's love? ...{37} But in all these things we have full victory through God who showed his love for us. {38-39} Yes, I am sure that nothing can separate us from the love God has for us. Not death, not life, not angels, not ruling spirits, nothing now, nothing in the future, no powers, nothing above us, nothing below us, or anything else in the whole world will ever be able to separate us from the love of God that is in Christ Jesus our Lord."

Nothing can separate you from God's love. Not even the following circumstances can do so.

1. Not the natural occurrences of life and the inevitability of death

2. Not your daily circumstances, both good and not good

3. Not supernatural beings, either good or evil

4. Not events now or in the future

5. Not anything or anyone in God's creation

Will you receive, cherish and hold tightly to God's love? Will you choose to be a vessel that pours out His kind of love with every chance you have to do so? Will you commit to a journey to discover who God is and what His kind of love means to you?

The journey always begins with a decision to follow Jesus. If you have not done so, or if you have not honored the prayer for salvation you once prayed, let this be your opportunity to commit to serving the God who loves you so much that He gave His only Son, to die for your redemption and eternal future. Let these words help you to make that commitment.

Father, in Jesus name, I repent of my sin of unbelief and of all that has offended You. I ask You to forgive me. I turn from my old ways and turn to the path You have called me to walk. I will love You, serve You, and follow You all the days of my life. Thank You for saving me, in Jesus' name. Amen.

Let me end with this thought. Fill your heart, your life's journey and your destiny with God's kind of love. Then, you will walk through all your days, listening with gladness, to your Savior's happy song of love, sung just for you.

Zephaniah 3:17 (NLT)

"For the LORD your God has arrived to live among you. He is a mighty savior. He will rejoice over you with great gladness. With his love, he will calm all your fears. He will exult over you by singing a happy song."

With every blessing, and a happy song from God,

Dr. Bob Abramson

About Dr. Bob Abramson

Dr. Abramson has extensive experience as a cross-cultural mentor and trainer of those in the five-fold ministry. He and his wife Nancy have pastored international churches in New York City and the Fiji Islands in the South Pacific. He established or taught in Bible schools and ministry training centers in New Zealand, Fiji, Taiwan, Hong Kong, Malaysia, Europe and the United States. He provides free resources worldwide through his website, "Mentoring Ministry" (www.mentoringministry.com).

Dr. Abramson earned a Doctor of Ministry from Erskine Theological Seminary, a Masters in Religion from Liberty University and a Bachelor of Arts in the Bible with a minor in Systematic Theology from Southeastern University. He and his wife Nancy live in Lake Worth, Florida. They have five grown children and six grandchildren.

Contact Dr. Abramson, at www.mentoringministry.com
or write him at Dr.Bob@mentoringministry.com

Dr. Abramson is also the author of these books.
- "Just a Little Bit More - The Heart of a Mentor" (Book and Workbook)
- "The Leadership Puzzle" (Two Workbooks and The Facilitator's Manual)
- "Growing Together, Marriage Enrichment for Every Culture." (Book and Workbook)
- "Reflections, Volumes One and Two," the first two in a series of devotional journals
- "Moral Manhood - Swimming with the Sharks"
- "Focus on the Father - The Lord's Prayers"

www.ingramcontent.com/pod-product-compliance
Lightning Source LLC
LaVergne TN
LVHW021504080426
835509LV00018B/2398